PRAISE FOR YVONNE CAMPER'S BOOK AND MINISTRY

Yvonne has a depth of insight, revelation, and perspective relating to the issues of those serving in leadership, particularly in the western church world. Her compelling prophetic insight, deep thought, personal conviction blended with a passion to see healthy leaders has motivated her to highlight this area. I believe what she shares in this book will prepare an emerging generation and empower existing leaders.

HOPE MOVEMENT -ARUBA
Dr. Linda Wallace
www.lindawallace.co

Between the Porch and the Altar Ministries is called out by God to minister to leaders for such a time as this. The founder, Yvonne D. Camper is passionate about touching the lives of those who are in the trenches of church life. She is serious about this work and does not mind laboring and travailing to bring about deliverance and change. Her goal is to please God and serve the people, while at the same time, loving her family, who labors with her. May God continue to empower her ministry!

"OH! SING PRAISES!"
Annette Hubbard, Author
www.abundanceofpraiseministries.org

Your book is very eye-opening. I've never read anything quite like it. I look forward to working with you again. Your work makes sense and has value.

CHRISTIAN WOMANHOOD MAGAZINE
Linda Stubblefield - Managing Editor
www. christianwomanhood.org

I highly recommend this book to anyone seeking insight into the mind of the prophet. This is a well-researched well-written book concerning guidelines for the life of the prophet. The information contained is biblically-based, spirit-inspired and written with prophetic vision. In many instances, it appears the subject matter is directed squarely at the life of the reader. Not only will it benefit prophets but is also applicable to anyone in the body of Christ seeking wisdom to manage the issues of life in a God-honoring, biblical manner.

ABUNDANT LIVING SCHOOL OF MINISTRY
Andre' Bryant – Instructor

Yvonne Camper was the Co-Chair of Mentorship for the national multi-cultural business resource group KP WELL – Kaiser Permanente Women Embracing Life and Leadership. From the first time, I met Yvonne at one of our events, I realized that here was someone with knowledge, experience and an energy to go after what she is passionate about. Shortly after that, I added to that assessment someone who follows through with action—effective and appropriate action. As the Chair of the Board, I know that I speak for all our members who will miss Yvonne's energy, enthusiasm, knowledge, and wit. I recommend her highly with no reservations.

KP WELL - KAISER PERMANENTE WOMEN EMBRACING LIFE AND LEADERSHIP
Pauline Field – KP WELL, Chair

I asked God to bring a Spirit-filled woman in my life who would help me heal from rejection issues, develop my gifts, and build my confidence. Since I have been working with Yvonne and the Holy Spirit I have grown spiritually, healed emotionally and physically. I am working through my issues and have lost close to seventy – pounds! I personally feel the weight was tied to my emotional issues. I now love myself and know how much I am loved by God.

TAKING MY TEMPLE BACK
Emma Aguirre, Founder

Yvonne Denise Camper is a Prophetic Voice, whose mission, mandate and Ministry helped save my life. I met Yvonne in 2016 and knew my day of deliverance was coming. If you have ever wrestled with your flesh, shame, and disgrace, then you know the inner turmoil it can cause. Between the Porch and the Altar Ministries spoke to the areas of pain no one else saw or was bold enough to confront. Through relationship building and consistent follow-up, I wasn't left to change my bandages. She is concerned with the heart and healing of the prophets as well as the people of God. She affirmed me and helped me unashamedly break cycles of legal trafficking. I can now say, "I am free, I am healed and I am dealing with my issues. For I am prophet that is not for profit."

TOUCH THE HEM INTERNATIONAL MINISTRIES

Shamilla Pennington, Founder
www.tthintlministries.org

Between the Porch and the Altar Ministries is conscientious about creating a safe, clean, non-judgmental and Holy Spirit-filled environment. The Spirit-led teachings have helped me in my prophetic journey and have given me practical lessons that I could immediately apply. I have been tremendously blessed and am grateful to be part of a group of people that are cheering me on so that I can be successful in Jesus.

SOUTH AFRICAN CONSULATE GENERAL

Renele Awono, Political Secretary,

Great writing! I enjoyed reading it. As a spiritual leader myself, I found it helpful. I could see the truth ringing through in many personal experiences I've seen, especially in the many broken families I've worked with.

PROFESSIONAL COUNSELOR

Scotty Brooks, M.Div.

I have known Yvonne Camper for over four years, and she is an answer to my prayers. I was seeking God for a mentor, and He sent her. She has truly been a blessing and has superseded the call of mentorship. Yvonne has taken on the role of spiritual mother, prayer warrior, encourager, marriage counselor, and teacher.

Also, Yvonne is one of the most-kind hearted people I have ever met. She always exhibits the fruit of the Holy Spirit, even during her own personal trials. Also, the way she flows in the gifts of the Holy Spirit and how she helps people is truly amazing. Yvonne loves God, and she loves people. She is my role model.

Furthermore, she has allowed me to become a part of her family, and I now call her mommy, since my natural mother is deceased. Yvonne is a woman of *character and integrity. Lastly, she is a great woman of God, a wife that honors her husband, a loving mother and a friend you can depend on.*

WIFE, MOTHER, AND AUTHOR

Taniysha MeBane

It is a very significant book, written in a simple, clear literary style, but with deep, insightful content. But what added further validity to your thoughts and ideas were the autobiographical references which were both revealing about yourself and at the same time relevant to the life of most of us who are your readers. Hence, we were not just reading good theoretical information but tested and proven experiences.

I was and am still struck by the profile painted of the prophet in Part One of the Text. It is not the traditional picture of the prophet, neither is it the popular concept of the prophetical role and personage. But the highlight of the Book for me was captured in Part Two where you treated the wounds with therapeutic precision. In a masterful and non-offensive manner, you applied the secular insights of others like Maslow to address the deep needs of the inner man.

Yes, you captured my interest throughout my journey home and within the confines of the aircraft I could not escape the compelling need for self-inspection and self-judgment, self-surrender the challenge to make it part of my life's journey.

It is an excellent book from an excellent lady, one of a kind, God's uniquely crafted prophetess, an example to the Body of Christ and a gift to every wounded prophet.

PROFESSOR AND INTERNATIONAL SPEAKER
Dr. C.B. Peter Morgan, D. Min, M.Div., B.A.

HEALING the WOUNDS

PROPHETIC LEADERSHIP TRANSFORMED

Yvonne D. Camper

ALTAR BOOKS
A DIVISION OF

QUIVERFULL
PUBLISHING

© 2017 by Yvonne D. Camper
Healing the Wounds; Prophetic Leadership Transformed

All rights reserved. No portion of this book may be reproduced, stored in a retrieval system, or transmitted in any form or by means-electronic, mechanical, photocopy, recording, scanning, or other-except for brief quotations in critical reviews or articles, without prior permission of the publisher.

Published in Fontana, California by Altar Books. Altar Books is a registered trademark of Quiver Full Publishing, Inc.

Altar Books titles may be purchased in bulk for educational, business, fundraising, or sales promotional use. For information, please e-mail *info@qfpublishing.com*

Unless otherwise noted, Scriptures used in this volume are taken from the Holy Bible, the New King James Version®. Copyright © 1982 by Thomas Nelson. Used by permission. All rights reserved.

Scriptures noted (NIV) are taken from the Holy Bible, New International Version®, NIV® Copyright ©1973, 1978, 1984, 2011 by Biblica, Inc.® Used by permission. All rights reserved worldwide.

Scriptures noted (GW) are taken from the Holy Bible, GOD'S WORD Translation, Copyright © 1995 by God's Word to the Nations. Used by permission of Baker Publishing Group.

Scriptures noted (ISV) are taken from the Holy Bible, International Standard Version, Copyright © 1995-2014 by ISV Foundation. All rights reserved internationally. Used by permission of Davidson Press, LLC.

Scriptures noted (NET) are taken from the Holy Bible, New English Translation, NET Bible® copyright ©1996-2006 by Biblical Studies Press, L.L.C. http://netbible.com All rights reserved.

Scriptures noted (LEB) are taken from the Holy Bible, Lexham English Bible, 2012 by Logos Bible Software. Lexham is a registered trademark of Logos Bible Software.

Scriptures noted (MSG) are taken from the Holy Bible, The Message, Copyright © 1993, 1994, 1995, 1996, 2000, 2001, 2002 by Eugene H. Peterson.

Scriptures noted (AMP) are taken from the Holy Bible, Amplified Bible, Copyright © 2015 by The Lockman Foundation, La Habra, CA 90631. All rights reserved.

Scriptures noted (NASB) are taken from the Holy Bible, New American Standard Bible, Copyright © 1960, 1962, 1963, 1968, 1971, 1972, 1973, 1975, 1977, 1995 by The Lockman Foundation.

Scriptures noted (NLT) are taken from the Holy Bible, New Living Translation, copyright © 1996, 2004, 2015 by Tyndale House Foundation. Used by permission of Tyndale House Publishers Inc., Carol Stream, Illinois 60188. All rights reserved.

Scriptures noted (EXB) are taken from the Holy Bible, The Expanded Bible, Copyright © 2011, Thomas Nelson Inc. All rights reserved.

Library of Congress Control Number: 2017937548

Paperback: ISBN 13: 978-0998-8391-0-3
          ISBN-10:0-9988391-0-8

E-book: ISBN-13:978-0-9988391-5-8

Printed in the United States of America

i

CONTENTS

FORWARD x
PREFACE xii
INTRODUCTION xvi
PART ONE: PRACTICAL PROPHETIC LIVING 1
WHAT IS A PROPHET? 2
HOW DO I KNOW IF I AM A PROPHET? 5
THE NEW TESTAMENT PROPHET 9
FALSE OR TRUE 11
THE PROPHETIC MINISTRY IN MOTION? 15
THE PROPER RESPONSE TO A PROPHETIC WORD 21
EMPOWERED BY THE HOLY SPIRIT 23
THE SPIRIT-FILLED CHURCH 26
PROPHET NOT FOR PROFIT 28
THE SIN OF DUPLICATION 31
WHOLE AND HOLY 33
PROPHETIC SEASONS 35
THE JEZEBEL FACTOR 38
PROPHETIC INCUBATION 44
OF MANTLE AND OF MEN 47
MANTLE READY 50
THE SPIRIT OF GAHAZI 53
WIRED TO BRING ORDER 55
INFALLIBLE 57
BUILT TO LAST 60
ADVANCING IN THE SPIRIT 63
THE ART OF THE APOTHECARY 64
THE MARKS OF A MATURE PROPHET 69
INHERENT QUALITIES 77

ARMED AND READY 80
MANAGING THE PROPHETIC FAMILY 82
MINISTERING TO THE PROPHETIC HUSBAND 84
SAFEGUARDING THE PROPHETIC CHILD 86
EXCELLING IN THE WORKPLACE 89
WITCHES IN THE WORKPLACE 92
A COMPANY OF PROPHETS 95
OPERATING IN PROPHETIC PRECISION 98
ESTABLISHING A PROPHETIC MINISTRY 105
PROPHETIC DREAMS AND VISIONS 107
PART TWO: HEALING THE WOUNDS 111
THE WOUND PRINCIPLE 112
ABANDONED 117
TRAUMATIZED 120
WHERE THE ENEMY TRAFFICS 126
EMOTIONAL BARRIERS 129
CHURCH HURT 130
MANAGING MINISTRY WOUNDS 133
THE WOUNDED PROPHET 136
AN ACCEPTABLE SACRIFICE 140
KILLING THE ROOT 142
THE WORKS OF THE FLESH 144
UNCLEAN LIPS 146
TESTED 148
THE STING OF BETRAYAL 151
PROPHETIC TRAINING 101 153
UNDERSTANDING REJECTION 155
CHARACTER OVER POWER 158
RECOVERING FROM GRIEF 160

THE CLEANSING OF THE PRIESTS	163
THE LEPER CHRONICLES	165
OFFENSES WILL COME	167
BLURRED LINES	169
DIVINE CORRECTION	171
A SPIRIT OF ANGER	174
PART THREE: LESSONS LEARNED	**177**
THE PROPHET'S CREED	178
LESSONS LEARNED	180
GOD'S NUMBER TWO MAN: AARON	181
COMMITTED TO THE CALL: AHIJAH	182
FULLY LOADED: ABRAHAM	183
THE POWER OF PROPHETIC OVERSIGHT: AGABUS	184
READY TO MOVE: AMOS	185
BRUISED BUT NOT BROKEN: ANNA	187
GOD HONORS RIGHTEOUSNESS: DANIEL	189
GOD'S LEADING LADY: DEBORAH	190
MENTAL EXHAUSTION: ELIJAH	192
GOD'S SUCCESSION PLAN: ELISHA	193
DELIVERING A DIFFICULT MESSAGE: EZEKIEL	194
A KEY TO GREAT LEADERSHIP: GAD	196
IT'S NOT FAIR: HABAKKUK	197
WORKING IN TANDEM: HAGGAI AND ZECHARIAH	199
A HOUSE IN ORDER: HEMAN AND SAMUEL	200
UNCOMMON OBEDIENCE: HOSEA	201
A TRUSTED PROFESSIONAL: HULDAH	203
PROPHETIC SCRIBES:	204
MINISTRY PREPARATION: ISAIAH	206
YOU ARE NEVER TOO YOUNG: JEREMIAH	208

A SEASON OF TESHUVA: JOEL 209
GOD IS SOVEREIGN: JOHN THE BAPTIST 211

ACKNOWLEDGEMENTS

It would be a travesty if I failed to acknowledge the John the Baptists of our generation and my spiritual mentors, Bishop Clarence McClendon, Pastors Owen and Audrey Black, Bishop Lamont and Pastor Anita Clayton, Apostle Ron Carpenter, Dr. Charles Martin and Dr. Charles Stanley, to whom I owe an eternal debt. Although my encounters with each of them were not always personal, just the impact of their ministries immensely affected my life.

They taught me how to have an excellent presentation, how to be healed, how to become acquainted with the anointing the Holy Spirit has given me, how to be transparent, how to manage a prophetic anointing, how to relentlessly pursue truth, how to be unyielding in my faith, how to submit to authority, how to have a firm foundation in the Word, how to live life in the Spirit, how to walk in the authority that Jesus has given every believer, the power of sowing and reaping, and the power of forgiveness. Without them, I would not be the woman I am today. I am forever grateful; you are truly gifts to the body of Christ.

To my dear husband who makes me laugh, gives me the space to create, breathe, and dream. I appreciate and thank you for allowing me to heal and for always having an open ear to listen.

To my five amazing children, (Brianne Sample, Roman, Zion, Christian, and Benjamin Styles), who have been so supportive of the ministry that God has given me to steward. You are some of the greatest servants in the body of Christ. Thank you for helping with every conference and event where you tirelessly served. Your support has been priceless.

To Anita Pollard, our lunchtime walks were more valuable than you will ever imagine. Thank you for letting me aspire, strategize, cry and prepare for the ministry. I value our friendship and appreciate all the times you encouraged me to be everything God created me to be.

DEDICATION

This book is dedicated to my mentee and spiritual son Arturo Da'Naire Frazier, a young prophet, who tragically lost his life after being hit by a car while leaving church. When I received the news, it was a brutal awareness that he was gone. I understood we would never have another conversation, and the reality of it left me devastated. Our connection was one-on-one and away from the pressures of ministry. Our bond was by divine decree. Therefore, I was unaware of the tremendous impact he had on the Kingdom of God and his community, until after his death. Over 2,500 people attended his funeral. It was standing room only.

He would often reach out to me for prophetic counsel but one morning, his face kept popping up in my dream, and the Holy Spirit told me to serve him and care for him. Now I understand why; he was in danger. He indeed was ordained, prophetic, gifted and serving humanity ran through his veins, but he was emotionally bankrupt, broken-hearted from ministry and ministering on a tank with no reserves.

I reached out to him and our Monday morning sessions began. My only concern for him was, "How was his heart? Which was always my pressing question to him. I appreciate the dedicated work he did towards his emotional health and healing. I will miss his smile, his compassionate heart, his enthusiasm for life, and Monday's will never be the same.

I am rejoicing now that he is with the greatest mentor in the universe! His text, emails, and letters will serve as a constant memory of his presence in my life. My last text to him was, "You are loved and appreciated," which I believe is the sentiment of all who knew him. Arturo was a force of nature; he did not just exist, He lived and still lives! He was far more impactful than he ever realized. It was a pleasure and an honor to serve him.

Arturo's life and legacy live on through the Arturo Da'Naire Scholarship Fund, where his mother and sister give annual scholarships to students towards their college education. I am a dedicated and committed Board Member and am proud to say, in

2018, we gave away $5,000 in scholarships. I love and miss him and can't wait to see him on Monday, in eternity. Please visit his website at www.adfscholarshipfund.org and generously give.

In closing, I extend a prayer for every prophetic leader and servant. I decree that you allow the Holy Spirit to give you rest in your soul. I decree that He revitalize you, reposition you, rejuvenate you and replenish you. You can't minister on fumes.

FOREWARD

Prophetess Yvonne Camper is a prophet of prophets. Her love for the office is felt deeply within the pages of this book. This publication breathes with her passion for ministry as she inspires us to take a deeper look at our ministerial sacrifices we offer to God.

This book is real, rare, and affectionately raw breaking down biblical truths and explaining with clarity the role of the prophet. This book is vital to those holding this office. If you are called to carry this critically important mantle, you are challenged to stay connected to God and committed to always keeping fresh oil in a time of great deception in the Body of Christ.

This book you are holding is truly a guide for those who carry the blessed call of the prophet, and a must-read for anyone desiring to understand himself or other prophets in a deeper way. Masterfully written with important wisdom nuggets oozing from each page, this is a book that will add value to your ministry library for many years to come.

Anesha Sharp, Author
Aneshasharp.com

PREFACE

The original meaning of the word "holocaust" was "burnt offering or sacrifice by fire." It was derived from the Greek word *holokauston*, which meant, "a thing wholly burnt." Jewish and biblical tradition signifies that the burnt offering had to be offered on the altar and be completely consumed by fire; nothing could remain. The meaning of the word was ultimately expanded in the 1670s to imply "a massacre" or "destruction of a large number of persons, especially by fire." As of 1957, the word was introduced into the English language in reference to the Nazi genocide of the European Jews.[1]

In the annals of history, the Holocaust was also known as the "Final Solution" and was the culmination of a decade-long impaction of the Nazi regime and policy; the goal was purification of the German race. For God's chosen people, Nazism was one of the gravest eras of human history and today; it still brings a sense of grief and sadness to those who were affected by it. Today, the effects and implications of the Jewish race are still profound and evident. Albeit, the current definition of the word is the point of reference for this book, the original Jewish and biblical usage will be expanded upon.

In the first act of worship following the flood, Noah built an altar and sacrificed animals and clean birds on it. God's response to Noah's sacrificial offering was a covenant with man that He would never curse the ground again (Genesis 8:20-21).

> *Then Noah built an altar to the Lord, and took of every clean animal and of every clean bird, and offered burnt offerings on the altar. And the Lord smelled a soothing aroma. Then the Lord said in His heart, 'I will never again curse the ground for man's sake, although the imagination of man's heart is evil from his youth; nor will I again destroy every living thing as I have done.*

The law of first mention deduces that the first occurrence of a principle in scripture establishes a fixed and unalterable blueprint for the interpretation of the scriptures going forward. Therefore, the inference can be made that the burnt offering was of the highest order of sacrificial offerings to the Lord.

Later in scripture, these offerings were commonly executed at the time of the morning and evening prayers. In the book of Leviticus, the principles and guidelines around the burnt offering were established. The laws and parameters inaugurated around the burnt offering or worship were extremely specific and had to be followed precisely.

According, to Leviticus 17:8,9, any violations were taken very seriously, and the penalties were costly. The Levitical Law states:

> *Also, you shall say to them: 'Whatever man of the house of Israel, or of the strangers who dwell among you, who offers a burnt offering or sacrifice, and does not bring it to the door of the tabernacle of meeting, to offer it to the LORD, that man shall be cut off from among his people.*

Nadab and Abihu (Leviticus 1:1, 2) refused to follow the protocol and offered a sacrifice so profane and offensive to God that they both were consumed by fire. The Bible uses the term "*strange fire*," which carries the connotation that it was "a sacrifice that God did not ask for or require." Their sacrifice was initiated by man.

The Holy Spirit spoke something vastly profound to me regarding the sacrificial offerings of the modern-day church. He said, "The death of the human spirit by strange fire has been a holocaust of epic proportions!"

When we offer sacrifices to God out of our fleshly desires, our worship is defective. God desires true worship and will not accept anything less. Warren Wiersbe wrote,

> True worship examines and exposes the depths of our being; God helps us see our true motives and values. In worship, God calls us to wholeness; but first, he must reveal our brokenness and our blemishes. He calls us to spiritual health, but first He must expose our 'wounds and bruises and putrefying sores' (Isaiah 1:6), and we can't go elsewhere for a second opinion.[2]

Faulty worship is profaning the sanctuary and massacring the people of God at lightning speed. The church is the only battalion that leaves its wounded, and hemorrhaging soldiers draped across the battlefield while turning a deaf ear and a blind eye to the devastation at hand. Unfortunately, this practice seems to be a common occurrence, and once the shock of it passes over, things return to business as usual. Regrettably, the world expects this kind of conduct from the church, and skeptical eyes are watching everywhere as these man-made empires rise and fall. The only concern appears to be the fear of losing it all, and priests scramble in desperation to hold onto the fleshly kingdoms that they have built.

This book is devoted to those whose sacrificial worship is pure and not desecrated by fleshly influence. These are those who must be the John the Baptists of their day, crying out in the wilderness, not bowing at the altar of human approval and not being afraid to rise above the fray of public opinion.

I believe, more than ever that God is calling the church back to the basic and simple principles of biblical worship. He is calling believers to worship Him absent of all the accouterments that have been established in modern-day agendas. He is moving Christians away from being seeker-sensitive and a watered-down Gospel that is the norm in today's American churches.

Continuing in this manner will create a generation of believers who desire entertainment more than they desire change. Crafting more and more, a culture of spiritual vagabonds who hop from church to church simply to seek their next fix. They are pious junkies desecrating their spiritual veins with contaminated worship.

As leaders, we are obligated to ensure that our quest for relevancy is not opening us to a spirit of deception. I believe the Lord is reminding us all that, *"For everything in the world—the lust of the flesh, the lust of the eyes, and the pride of life—comes not from the Father but from the world"* (1 John 2:16, NIV).

INTRODUCTION

It was an evening service at The Church of the Harvest, circa 1992. I had already attended the morning service and had sung in the choir for three services; I felt extremely tired. But when the prophet said that we needed to get back to church that night because there was a word from the Lord, my spirit responded with a hearty "Yes!" and "Amen!" because I knew it was something that I could not miss. My encounter with the prophetic message that night was life-altering; I remember the night as if it were yesterday.

I could absolutely feel in the atmosphere that something was about to change for me; I somehow knew that I would never be the same. The prophet began to minister and said, "None of you are here by accident." I do not recall all who were in the room with me, but I am sure they had the same experience that I did. It spiritually stabilized me in a way I had not experienced up until that point. During that season in my life, my biggest fear was missing God. That night settled the matter forever.

On the way home, my body was shaking so heavy under the anointing I could barely drive. I worshiped and cried the entire way home. The heavenly melody which I heard playing on the piano and the prophet's declaration was still crystal-clear in my mind. His words shaped and patterned the ministry I would later steward. He said,

> What scares me is the possibility of having a big thing going and not realizing we lost God somewhere. Preachers die, and churches perish trying to sustain by human intervention what was birthed by divine inspiration. Men fall apart trying to hold together by human ingenuity what only the Holy Spirit could orchestrate.
>
> None of it means anything if the presence of God leaves when you come off the pulpit. What is it that if God gave it to you, would challenge His place in your heart? What is it that would rival your affection for God if you had it? Is having the presence of God more important to you than anything else?

We must want His presence more than fame, notoriety or popularity. Prosperity and success are a dangerous thing if your heart is not fixed or in the right place. People have gone into Canaan and self-destructed because their heart was not fixed on God.[3]

Prophetic pioneer, please do not allow yourself to be destroyed because of the goodness of God. Don't allow your ministry to cower under the weight of sinful desires and pleasures. Keep your heart wholly devoted to Him. For the Lord has need of thee.

PART ONE
PRACTICAL PROPHETIC LIVING

Reminiscent of a time when everything sacred was written and everything written was sacred - Unknown

1

WHAT IS A PROPHET?

A prophetic gift in its purest form is a reformer; the voice of God in the earth, a mouthpiece, a firebrand, a spokesperson inspired to teach or proclaim the will of God, God's representative and ambassador. Paul, the Apostle, wrote in Ephesians 4:11,12:

And He Himself gave some to be apostles, some prophets, some evangelists, and some pastors and teachers, for the equipping of the saints for the work of ministry, for the edifying of the body of Christ.

At this juncture in biblical history, Jesus had descended into the bowels of the earth, was positioned to ascend far above the heavens to sit at the right hand of the Father and was in the process of discharging His earthly duties. During His ministry, He embodied all five gifts, but now these gifts needed to be distributed across the body in His absence. These gifts would be deposited in the spirits of men and women under the governance of the Holy Spirit to expand the reach of His church.

All the gifts are needed and necessary for the church to be operating at full throttle and on all cylinders, but the prophetic gift impacts the church in a significant way. Prophets are extremely discerning, charismatic and very persuasive; which can be why Jesus is urging believers in the last days to be aware of false prophets (Matthew 7:15).

Resident in the prophetic gift is the power to move the church exponentially forward. Prophets, who are the eyes and the defining voice of the church, are used by God to build up and mature His people. They are not called by men but are sanctioned and ordained in the womb of their mothers; men can only affirm and recognize the gift.

God spoke to Jeremiah in Jeremiah 1:5 and said, *"Before I formed you in the womb I knew you; Before you were born I sanctified you; I ordained you a prophet to the nations."* This passage confirms your very call. Even before you were born, God consecrated and appointed you for service. The word "knew" comes from the Hebrew word *Yada*,[4] which surmises God was intimate and well acquainted with your purpose long before you were ever conceived.

I want to clarify that simply prophesying does not make a person a prophet. There is a vast difference between the gift of prophecy and the office of the prophet. The Holy-Spirit-administered gift in 1 Corinthians 12:10 is distributed as He, the Holy Spirit, wills. The distribution of these gifts is based on the present need and circumstances of the church.

The office of a prophet, on the other hand, is a stationary position in the body of Christ whose function goes far beyond prophesying. The office gifting tends to be more administrative and jurisdictional in nature. A spiritual governance accompanies the office, and they are assigned to certain territories and people. One of my mentors told me that the responsibility of a prophet is to control the spiritual traffic of the regions and or territories in which they have been assigned.

The Holy Spirit spoke to me one day and said, "I don't assign you to churches; I assign you to people." This instruction gave me more clarity and understanding of how I was supposed to position myself organizationally in the local church.

I have been a member of five local churches in my thirty years of ministry. Regardless of how I try to remain inconspicuous, prophets always seem to gravitate towards me, which creates an opportunity for me to serve. At a previous church where I served, there were over 10,000 members. My goal was to be ministered to and replenished, but God's plan was for me to release the healing anointing to the prophets that had been praying and waiting for my arrival. Young prophet, understanding you do not have to make yourself known is important. God will always alert someone of your presence. Sit, worship, and be faithful until He opens a door for service.

Additionally, it is important to recognize that when we are functioning as prophets, we have not been sent to undermine the authority of the church. We function prophetically as the Lord opens doors and under the auspices of appointed leadership. You have authority where you have responsibility. If the leadership is resistant to the call, then prayer and dedicated service must be your recourse until God speaks to those in authority.

2

HOW DO I KNOW IF I AM A PROPHET?

1 John 2:20-21 (KJV) says, *"But ye have an unction from the Holy One, and ye know all things. I have not written unto you because ye know not the truth, but because ye know it, and that no lie is of the truth."* This passage refers to discerning the truth from error in relation to the person of Jesus Christ, but I think it is relevant to help us understand that the Holy Spirit gives us all the information we need concerning who we are. The Greek word for unction is *charisma*,[5] which means to "anoint with oil." In the Old Testament, God's chosen one would be physically anointed with oil to symbolize that God's hand was on him. *Anoint*[6] for us refers "to the teaching and gifting ministry of the Holy Spirit, guiding the receptive believer into the fullness of God's preferred-will."[7]

One of the ways you know you are a prophet is because the Holy Spirit tells you. I have met so many people who, when I start discussing the prophetic ministry, something in them is quickened. God is faithful in directing and guiding His people. Let Him confirm the gift; it is not His nature to leave a person ignorant.

The scriptures indicate God's initial contact with a prophet is through the medium of dreams and visions as recorded in Numbers 12:6, which says, *"Hear now My words: If there is a prophet among you, I, the LORD, make Myself known to him in a vision; I speak to him in a dream."* Very early on, many prophets have an extremely active and vivid dream life where specific details can be clearly remembered. These are not the only signs, but I believe the most common. My dreams as a child were very vibrant. I also frequently experienced what the world calls déjà vu; I always had the feeling that I had been somewhere before. I now understand as a budding prophet that I saw things in the spirit realm before I was seeing them in the natural.

As already mentioned, God initially visits prophets in dreams and visions to train them to understand the supernatural and become familiar with His voice. There have been many times God has given me information that I would not have otherwise known. I do understand that He is always teaching me how to legally access the supernatural and deepen my understanding that everything seen exists in some form in the earth or spirit realm. It simply may not be known to me, but the Holy Spirit makes all things known in His purpose. In a later chapter, I will explain the purpose of dreams and visions. I will also equip you with tools on how to manage them effectively and biblically.

Another aspect of a prophetic gift is that you are very aware there is a spiritual realm. As a child, I was neither reared in a church nor had I accepted Christ. I also had no understanding of spiritual matters, but I felt extremely spiritual. I often felt God's presence and spent long hours talking to a God whom I had never formally met, and I often had encounters with demonic spirits or people influenced by them.

Without the required and necessary training, the prophetic gift can also cause great mental and emotional instability. Seeing things, you do not want to see and receiving information you do not know how to use can torment a prophet. When my gift began to flourish, I felt extremely confused and overwhelmed. It was not until a seasoned prophet took me under her wing and began to train me that everything I was experiencing started making sense.

The prophet can also become deceived and direct his quest for a spiritual connection toward unauthorized and illegal access of the spiritual realm. Because I was not reared in the church, my prophetic gift was very misguided. I used it to summon demonic spirits, tell fortunes, and chart my life through horoscopes.

I was also fascinated with Greek mythology and Ouija boards. I was completely oblivious to the spiritual doors I was opening or the damage I was doing to my soul.

My mother was a prophet, but because the office or the gifting was not understood at that time, nor were we regular churchgoers, instead of going to God she sought the advice of mediums. This behavior opened the door to mental illness. I have an extremely dramatic memory of my mother's nervous breakdown and demonic possession. The scriptures provide examples of the way demonic spirits can attack people, which include physical illness, mental anguish, the spread of false doctrine, spiritual warfare and for an unsaved person through possession.

Many who call themselves psychics can potentially embody the office of a prophet; the gift is present, but where a person seeks his information will determine for whom he is working. Psychics receive their information from the spirit of divination, which is witchcraft; prophets receive their information from the Holy Spirit for building up God's people as documented in 1 Corinthians 14:3,4, *"But he who prophesies speaks edification and exhortation and comfort to men. He who speaks in a tongue edifies himself, but he who prophesies edifies the church."*

Recently, I have heard the expression "church witch" several times; this is a self-refuting term. You cannot be part of the church and be a witch. These people are unregenerate and controlled by demonic influences to undermine authority, advance their agendas and thwart the progression of the ministry. These individuals need to be cast out and removed from the premises once you identify them. When you do that, everything and everyone attached to them will follow.

It is of great importance for a prophet to understand, as early as possible, what his biblical function is because the attack of the enemy can be debilitating if not recognized. I find in speaking with many prophets throughout my ministry that they all seemingly experienced excessive painful rejection and mental torment in their childhood. In my experience, many prophets, myself included, have experienced some form of sexual or physical abuse. My step-father hated me. He would frequently put me on punishment and beat me with an extension cord until my skin broke. I am clear now; the spirit of Herod was trying to destroy me emotionally and spiritually before I received the revelation of who I was.

Understanding who you are prevents prophets from using their gifts to destroy themselves or drive people away from God. The prophet's primary function is to drive people toward Him. This society is replete with spiritual experiences that do not include God, and people are desperately seeking answers to life's pressing questions. Sound advice reminds us God does not give a prophet information to harm people but gives them information to bring healing, holiness, wholeness, clarity, and reconciliation.

Last, of all, the prophetic walk is characterized by loneliness. Growing up, I could not understand why I never seemed to fit in; I always felt like a square peg in a round hole. God, of course, will surround a prophet with people who love him, but the prophet will never be part of the "in-crowd." In almost every biblical encounter, the environments to which prophets were called were often hostile. The people had no concern or desire to hear, let alone obey the voice of the Lord.

3

THE NEW TESTAMENT PROPHET

Some specific elements govern the New Testament prophet because, with the advent of the Holy Spirit, every believer has access to divine direction and information. When a New Testament prophet prophesies, he is corroborating what God has already spoken to a person. Many times, the word is *confirmation* more than it is *information*. For the New Testament prophets, life is not as rigorous as it was for their Old Testament counterparts; however, the prophetic assignment remains a responsibility that cannot be forfeited and a burden you must carry.

In the Old Testament, the prophets governed the nation and the people by the written law. Their primary responsibility was to announce warnings and judgments at the command of the Lord. They stood alone and answered only to God. Grace drives the New Testament prophets, and their focus is to strengthen and encourage the church. One of the primary responsibilities of a New Testament prophet is to create avenues where people can be reconciled to God. The Apostle Paul wrote 2 Corinthians 5:18, *"Now all things are of God, who has reconciled us to Himself through Jesus Christ, and has given us the ministry of reconciliation…"* Prophesying by itself is insufficient if a person does not move into a deeper relationship with God.

Moreover, the New Testament prophet answers not only to God but the church. They must embrace the fact that they are part of the church and are not supposed to be *"lone rangers."* Prophet Kris Vallotton said, "The day of ministering to the church and not being a part of it is over."

God spoke to me a few years back and told me to, "Go get the prophets in the highways and the byways." Since then, I have met so many prophets who do not have a home church. I believe there are three main reasons why. First, many have been hurt and offended by the church, and a church wound is very painful. They stay away because they are preserving themselves and do not trust that God can protect them. Second, they tend to see more than most people; because of this a prophet can become very prideful and arrogant and conclude that fellowship with other saints is no longer important or required. Finally, the prophet can be in complete rebellion against God and will reject all sound doctrine or instructions. Therefore, as a New Testament prophet, God desires that you stay connected to the body.

4

FALSE OR TRUE

How to tell the difference between a false prophet and a true prophet of God is a question that most people are interested in having answered. Initially, the Bible warns us in Matthew 7:15-16 (AMP),

> *Beware of the false prophets, [teachers] who come to you dressed as sheep [appearing gentle and innocent], but inwardly are ravenous wolves. By their fruit, you will recognize them [that is, by their contrived doctrine and self-focus].*

False prophets are those who have been called or commissioned by God and have chosen to operate in error and flesh. If the prophet is false, there must have been an element of truth that existed at one point in his life. One of the initial ways to identify a true prophet of God is whether you can sense a strong, identifiable presence of the Holy Spirit's ministry in their lives, which manifests itself in love and humility. The arrogance and pride of a false prophet can be cut with a knife. They are very extravagant, self-serving, and self-absorbed. They only use the anointing to captivate crowds and profit from the people's desire to hear from God. False prophets always prey on the weak, destitute and broken.

When a true prophet leaves your presence, the only thing you will remember is the message. A true prophet will never distract from the presence of God. A false prophet is very eloquent in speech and will make sure you remember his name. On Judgement Day, they will still be pleading their case. Matthew 7:22 (NIV) says, *"Many will say to me on that day, 'Lord, Lord, did we not prophesy in your name and in your name, drive out demons and in your name, perform many miracles?"*

A well-known pastor remembers when he was younger that the message of a visiting evangelist captivated his soul. He went up to the evangelist after the service and told him how amazing his message was and how his words impacted his life. The evangelist answered, "What are you going to do about it?" and walked away. That evangelist had no intention of rattling off his pedigree or making a personal connection. His only assignment was to make a divine deposit.

A true prophet only cares about how his message impacts his listeners, and the source is always the Word of God. His message will never deviate from it, and it is not full of his opinion. A false prophet funnels messages from a spirit of divination and will always twist the Word of God to fit his evil agenda. A red flag for me is when a prophet uses the Word of God sparingly or lacks the revelation to expound upon it. Deep and clever sayings are not always in line with biblical truths.

Additionally, people tend to think that because a false prophet can accurately tell someone his name, address, or phone number that he is a prophet of God. That person may have a prophetic gift, but the Holy Spirit is not always the source of his information; rather, familiar spirits are generally the culprits behind these operations. False prophets will progressively lead people away from God, making them trust in the word of a man, rather than the word of the Lord.

The accuracy of a word does not confirm that a message came from God. Fortune tellers, familiar spirits, soothsayers, and horoscopes can also be accurate. The test of true prophecy is time. The Bible says in 1 Samuel 3:19 (NIV), the Lord "...*let none of Samuel's words fall to the ground.*" Authentic prophecy will come to pass *and* move believers into a deeper, more intimate relationship with God, resulting in spiritual maturity. Just as a natural parent will not give his child anything he wants, God will not give His children everything they desire. He only releases those things that agree and are in synergistic alignment with His divine purpose and will for a person's life.

If a person is not careful, the words of false prophets can open the door for a spirit of lust, giving an individual, the impression God makes Himself available to fulfill their fleshly desires. It will make a person think that God is more interested in their personal advancement than He is in building His own kingdom.

The present religious culture treats prophecy like a cheap replication of fortune telling *by* paying prophets for a word. You cannot seek prophecy; prophecy seeks you. A believer's proper posture is and will always be to seek God—not gifts or power. These days, falling into the snares of cunning and deceptive false prophets is incredibly easy. Their god is their belly (Philippians 3:19), and they use their gifts for their own personal satisfaction and ill-gotten gain. The Bible adamantly warns believers against the ministry of the false prophet in the following passages:

> *Son of man, prophesy against the prophets of Israel who prophesy, and say to those who prophesy out of their own heart, 'Hear the word of the LORD!' Thus, says the Lord GOD: "Woe to the foolish prophets, who follow their spirit and have seen nothing!* (Ezekiel 13:2, 3).

The most defining factor in making the delineation between a false prophet and a true prophet is the life they live. A true prophet's life is in order and exemplifies godly character. When I say order, I am not insinuating perfection, but I am referring to a person who carries the heart of God and uses the Word of God as the guidepost. What a person does is far more important than what he says. Because a true mature prophet conveys the heart of God, he possesses an above average ability to manifest the love of God to His people (Romans 5:5). Satan can duplicate and mimic everything in the kingdom except the true conversion of a saint.

Since we all have been given the ministry of reconciliation as previously mentioned, prophets cannot be high on judgment and low on mercy, this does not include the times a prophet is instructed by God to bring a strong exhortative word nor does it mean to excuse sin. Romans 6:1 (NIV) says, *"What shall we say, then? Shall we go on sinning so that grace may increase?"*

Because we are New Testament believers and we have the infilling of the Holy Spirit, the final test is trusting the Spirit of God. He will not allow you to be deceived. Many are deceived because they desire something more than the will of God. They have what the Bible refers to as "itching ears." Paul wrote to Timothy, *"For the time will come when people will not put up with sound doctrine. Instead, to suit their desires, they will gather around them a great number of teachers to say what their itching ears want to hear"* (2 Timothy 4:3, NIV).

PRACTICAL PROPHETIC LIVING

Prophet of God, your life is the message, and living a life of holiness is an absolute necessity. Because of the magnitude in which your prophetic anointing affects the lives of God's people, it is imperative that the fruit of the Spirit flows through your life like an illimitable river. The prophet's life should be a constant exercise in manifesting the love of God.

5

THE PROPHETIC MINISTRY IN MOTION?

The prophetic ministry is a continuation and perpetuation of the ministry of Jesus Christ. Prophets are not the center of what they do; rather, they are part of the body. Separate and apart from the body, prophets are insignificant. 1 Corinthians 12:12 admonishes, *"For as the body is one and has many members, but all the members of that one body, being many, are one body, so also is Christ."* Prophets are part of a supernatural network, and the purpose of the church is to be a convergence zone for all the gifts so that the body of Christ can be fully operative and enriched. Understanding the prophetic ministry is to watch how Jesus guided the burgeoning church and confronted demonic spirits.

One of the fundamental roles of a prophet is to declare divinely inspired utterances through the channels of prophecy, words of wisdom or words of knowledge. Therefore, a biblical prophet is given the charge to stand as a spokesperson and herald a message on behalf of God. Prophets set forth standards of righteousness, confront the heresies of the day, and declare the truth and will of God concerning the church. A prophet's statements always contain the intent of God's heart for His people. These duties culminate in the prophet's life as a staunch defender of the faith. In response to false teachers Jude addressed his fellow believers in Jude 1:3 (NIV) saying, *"Dear friends, although I was very eager to write to you about the salvation we share, I felt compelled to write and urge you to contend for the faith that was once for all entrusted to God's holy people."*

At times, delivering the word of the Lord to an individual can be intimidating because the prophet can never be sure how the recipient will react. The person has a choice to accept or reject the message. Ultimately, he is not accepting or rejecting the prophet. Instead, He is accepting or rejecting God. The person's response is never personal.

A prophetic friend of mine delivered a message to a family for whom she was caring, and they responded, "We decided not to receive your words," although everything that she declared came to pass. A person receiving or rejecting the word does not diminish the potency or accuracy of the word God has given the prophet. Jesus commanded His disciples in Matthew 10:14 (NIV), *"If anyone will not welcome you or listen to your words, leave that home or town and shake the dust off your feet."*

It is important for a prophet to understand that when the Lord speaks to him and tells him to speak, it is not optional. It is not a suggestion but a command. A prophet must have the courage to speak as the oracle of God while divorcing himself from the response of people. The word must be spoken in the precise manner, in the precise place, to the precise person at the precise time. When delivering a message say what God is saying, no more and no less. You must resist the temptation to embellish a word to sound deep.

I was preparing to speak at a conference, and as I was seeking God for direction, the Holy Spirit spoke to me that someone would be dealing with issues related to fertility. Before delivering the message, I was a little hesitant to speak it because upon entering the conference room, I noticed it was filled with older women. Their interest in having a baby was very unlikely. As I began to speak, the word of the Lord came to me again; so, I spoke it as the Holy Spirit instructed me. Everyone looked around, and no one responded. I have learned to trust the Holy Spirit regardless of what the natural circumstances dictate. I have also matured to the place that I would rather speak it and be wrong than not speak it and have someone miss his or her opportunity in God.

After the conference, a woman came to me and said, "I have two children, but I am getting remarried. My fiancé and I want to have a child, but I have endometriosis." I knew that endometriosis is a disease, which causes the tissue that normally lines the uterus to grow outside of the uterus. The result is severe pain and infertility. I laid hands on her womb and commanded it to come into alignment with the word the Holy Spirit had spoken to me. I may never again see this woman, but I believe by faith the word of the Lord will be performed because He spoke it—not because I heard it.

In my earlier years, I attended a Benny Hinn Crusade, and there was a man sitting in front of me. The Holy Spirit instructed me to put my hands on his shoulders and pray because the man was in a state of unbelief. I was too afraid to respond that after the service was over, I tried to find him and couldn't. The Holy Spirit spoke to me and said, "It is important to obey at that moment because you may never get another opportunity to change a person's life if you ignore the first directive."

In another instance, on a prayer line, a woman asked for agreement concerning the impending miscarriage of her second child. She said, "I have been in and out of the hospital to prevent this miscarriage from happening." We prayed, and the word of the Lord came and said, "Do not fear; your cervix will remain closed."

A week later she was rushed to the hospital with contractions and severe distress. The physician's report said, "Your uterus is under distress, but your cervix is closed." I am overjoyed to say that a few months later, she delivered a beautiful baby girl who is now about two years old at the time this book is being written. Consequently, we must trust the Holy Spirit more than we trust our feelings, or people can miss the hand of the Lord operating in their lives. I am not saying people cannot get the information elsewhere, but I believe if God sends them to you, you have their word of deliverance.

I have found that when it is God, the word continues to agitate me until I release it. The caveat to this is we must be careful not to over-prophesy. Sometimes, a prophet can allow himself to be an instrument of the enemy by simply saying whatever comes to his mind and labeling it as *prophecy*. Contrary to popular belief, prophets prophesy infrequently as opposed to a daily or weekly occurrence. Scriptural references show that prophets did not prophesy all that much. So, a prophet must make sure that what he is saying to people is truly inspired by the Holy Spirit. Also, a prophet can misconstrue a word of wisdom or a word of knowledge for a prophetic word. Therefore, he must guard himself against becoming intoxicated with his gift.

I have been in ministries that believe a prophet can prophesy on the spot and seemingly everyone in the ministry has a prophetic word. The public gift of tongues and interpretation is very closely related to the gift of prophecy. Paul's biblical instruction was that there should be two or three prophets at the most speaking in a public setting. 1 Corinthians 14:27-29 says,

> *If anyone speaks in a tongue, let there be two or at the most three, each in turn, and let one interpret. But if there is no interpreter, let him keep silent in church, and let him speak to himself and God. Let two or three prophets speak, and let the others judge.*

When there is more than two or three, it is spiritual frenzy and chaos. Being a part of such a ministry can be extremely dangerous for new believers because they will begin to rely more on the prophet's word than the Word of God. They will rely on emotionalism rather than authentic ministry. It is important for prophets to teach people not to be reliant on them but dependent on the Holy Spirit and God's timeless Word.

The prophetic responsibility will include building and governing morality. Jeremiah 1:10 exemplifies the prophetic mandate: *"God said 'See, I have this day set you over the nations and over the kingdoms, to root out and to pull down, to destroy and to throw down, to build and to plant.'"* God sends prophets to the scene when it's the appointed time to build up or tear down a work.

Also, the following gifts, which are given by the Holy Spirit, regularly operate through their ministries:

- o **Words of Wisdom:** These inspired utterances give the person receiving the word a supernatural perspective along with divine information and authority to accomplish the will of God in a specific situation. The knowledge communicated is not earthly wisdom but a supernatural discharge of verifiable information, which enables the skillful application of knowledge.

- o **Words of Knowledge:** This is closely related to words of wisdom. A word of knowledge is revealed to a prophet by the Spirit. It is the ability to be able to ascertain what God is presently doing or intends to do in a person's life. Words of knowledge only provide information with no divine instruction. For that reason, words of knowledge must work conjointly with words of wisdom. When a prophet can reveal an individual's personal information, it is an example of words of knowledge in operation. A prophet uses this example to alert a person that God's Spirit is present, but in and of itself, it is useless information.

- **Discerning of Spirits:** This supernatural ability to discern and uncover the operatives of human and demonic spirits allows the prophet to identify whether a person is being influenced by the Holy Spirit or demonic forces. It also helps you understand the motives and intentions of people's hearts. This gift in operation is key to fulfilling one's destiny as demonic spirits operating through people are consistently at work in frustrating the plan of God in a person's life. Paul said in 1 Corinthians 16:9, *"For a great and effective door has opened to me, and there are many adversaries."* Paul would have been unable to discern adversarial opposition without the gift of discernment.

- **Healings and Miracles:** These are supernatural manifestations of God's healing power. A *healing* is "a progressive act of restoration," It is the Holy Spirit's sovereign intervention accompanied with divine instruction. A *miracle* is instantaneous and overrides natural time constraints. Miracles manifest as a testament to the glory of God and to authenticate the Holy Spirit's present authority.

In Acts 3:2-10, the man at the Gate Beautiful wanted money, but instead, his ability to walk was restored. The Bible says he entered the temple jumping and praising God, and the people were amazed and filled with wonder. We can ascertain from this passage that the prophet's only responsibility is to deliver the word of the Lord. He is not bound by the responsibility of making sure people receive it.

PRACTICAL PROPHETIC LIVING

Another key principle to grasp is that prophets are called to every walk of life and can operate outside of the church setting. The burden determines the responsibility. Martin Luther King, Jr., carried a burden for social change and racial injustice; therefore, he did not spend countless hours inside the four walls of a building but out in the streets as one crying out in the wilderness for justice and equality.

In closing this chapter, I want to address one of the most common assaults against the prophetic ministry in today's churches. Many believe that the function of the prophet has ceased. However, according to New Testament accounts (Matthew 23:34, Luke 2:36, Acts 21:9, and Romans 12:4-6), the gift is alive and well! Unfortunately, most churches have no room for the ministry of the prophet regardless of how vital this function is to the health, success, and vigor of the ministry. For the church to successfully fulfill its mission, the prophetic gift must work in synergy with the other gifts given by the resurrected and ascended Christ. Our prayer is that the church does not become a "non-prophet" organization.

6

THE PROPER RESPONSE TO A PROPHETIC WORD

The initial response to a prophetic word is to judge it by the Holy Spirit. As discussed previously, a word from a prophet is generally a confirmation of what God has already spoken to a person. Although, there are times when the word spoken by a prophet can be *information*. When that happens to me, my rule of thumb is I rarely reject a message from a prophet I trust; the operative word is *trust*. A trusted prophet is one whose ministry and life have been proven and verified. I also wait patiently for the Holy Spirit to confirm the message. If it is a word from the Lord, I will receive confirmation from two or three outside sources. Paul, the apostle, wrote in 2 Corinthians 13:1 (NIV), *"Every matter must be established by the testimony of two or three witnesses."*

A person's secondary and key response is to declare it and speak it until it manifests in the earth or he has a divine unction in his spirit that the matter is settled. Whenever a prophecy is given, it is given with the end in mind. Declaring the prophetic word is not so it will come to pass but it is to help you remain in a position of faith. Paul reminded the Corinthians that the catalyst to their faith was persistently listening to the word of God (Romans 10:17). Also, 2 Peter 1:19 (NIV) reminds us, *"We also have the prophetic message as something completely reliable, and you will do well to pay attention to it, as to a light shining in a dark place."*

Next, position yourselves to respond offensively to the enemy's attack because every word spoken will be tested. Be certain that you understand your life is hidden in Christ (Colossians 3:3); the angels of the Lord are encamped around you (Psalm 34:7), and no weapon formed against you will prosper (Isaiah 54:17). The purpose of prophecy is to arm you with weapons to overcome demonic strategies and attacks; it makes you battle-ready.

Prophecy champions the citizens of the kingdom and progressively moves them toward their divine purpose, but it will not happen without a fight!

PRACTICAL PROPHETIC LIVING

Mrs. Charles E. Cowman, the author of *Streams in the Desert,* wrote the following about spiritual warfare:

> It has often been said that a dispirited army goes forth to battle with the certainty of being beaten. We heard a missionary say recently that she had been invalided at home purely because her spirit had fainted, with the consequence that her body sunk also. We need to understand more of these attacks of the enemy upon our spirits and how to resist them. If the enemy can dislodge us from our position, then he seeks to "wear us out" (Daniel 7:25) by a prolonged siege, so that at last we, out of sheer weakness, let go the cry of victory.[8]

Paul told Timothy: *"This charge I commit to you, son…according to the prophecies previously made concerning you, that by them you may wage a good warfare"* (1 Timothy 1:18). In addition, prophecy is not for the gain of the prophet but is a tool to build up the body of Christ. Once again Paul is admonishing the church;

> *But when a person speaks what God has revealed, he speaks to people to help them grow, to encourage them, and to comfort them. When a person speaks in another language, he helps himself grow. But when a person speaks what God has revealed, he helps the church grow.* (1 Corinthians 14:3, 4, GW).

1 Corinthians 14:3 states, *"He who prophesies speaks edification and exhortation and comfort unto men."* If the prophetic word spoken to you does not contain any of these elements, then it probably isn't from God. A true prophetic word will always come to pass and be confirmed.

7

EMPOWERED BY THE HOLY SPIRIT

Since a prophet's main responsibility is to accurately deliver the word of the Lord, he must have a deep abiding fellowship and communion with the Holy Spirit. A prophet must have conviction, be holy, operate in power, be consecrated and be sanctified. These characteristics can only be birthed in an individual by the Word and the Holy Spirit. 2 Peter 1:21 says, *"For prophecy never came by the will of man, but holy men of God spoke as they were moved by the Holy Spirit,"* and 1 Samuel 10:6 (KJV) says, *"And the Spirit of the LORD will come upon thee, and thou shalt prophesy with them, and shalt be turned into another man."* The scriptures give a clear indication that prophets are moved by God's Spirit to utter divine messages to His people.

In the Old Testament, God's spirit had not yet embodied a believer; nonetheless, prophets, priests, and kings were heavenly inspirited by Him. The Old Testament term is *"The Spirit of God came upon them."* They were not even able to speak without being moved by Him.

In the New Testament, the Holy Spirit is the only person, after Jesus, in the Godhead who is speaking and is in full operation. He lives inside of believers and has been given to them as a down payment of their future salvation (Ephesians 1:13, 14) as well as empowering them for service (Acts 1:8).

Jesus was the One who championed His arrival as He comforted His disciples regarding His imminent departure. In John 14:15-18 saying:

> *If you love Me, keep My commandments. And I will pray the Father, and He will give you another Helper, that He may abide with you forever—the Spirit of truth, whom the world cannot receive, because it neither sees Him nor knows Him; but you know Him, for He dwells with you and will be in you. I will not leave you orphans; I will come to you.*

PRACTICAL PROPHETIC LIVING

In another account, Jesus was speaking to His disciples on the threshold of Pentecost and on the precipice of the New Testament church in Luke 24:49 (KJV). He said, *"And, behold, I send the promise of my Father upon you: but tarry ye in the city of Jerusalem, until ye be endued with power from on high."* Even before Jesus' ministry, Luke 3:21 says the Holy Spirit descended upon Him like a dove. It is interesting to note that Jesus did not work one miracle before His encounter with the Holy Spirit.

If Jesus and the disciples needed the Holy Spirit to conduct ministry, how much more do the prophets need Him now because ministry without Him is ineffective, powerless, unproductive and merely fortune telling.

Moreover, in the book of Acts 19:11 it is documented how God worked unusual miracles by the hand of Paul. Prior to his working of miracles, the Bible documents his infilling of the Holy Spirit in Acts 9:17 (NIV), which says:

> *Then Ananias went to the house and entered it. Placing his hands on Saul, he said, "Brother Saul, the Lord—Jesus, who appeared to you on the road as you were coming here—has sent me so that you may see again and be filled with the Holy Spirit."*

Hence, a New Testament prophet being filled with the Holy Spirit is a mandate and not an option. So now, we know who the Holy Spirit is, but what does He do? As the heir of the New Testament church, He convicts the world of sin, righteousness, and judgment (John 16:8). Without Him, we lack the power to change. David's prayer was, *"Cast me not away from thy presence; and take not thy holy spirit from me"* (Psalm 51:11, KJV). Even in the Old Testament, David knew that God's presence in his life was key to his spiritual existence. 1 Corinthians 12:4-11 outlines His function in the New Testament church:

> *There are diversities of gifts, but the same Spirit. There are differences of ministries, but the same Lord. And there are diversities of activities, but it is the same God who works all in all. But the manifestation of the Spirit is given to each one for the profit of all: for to one is given the word of wisdom through*

> *the Spirit, to another the word of knowledge through the same Spirit, to another faith by the same Spirit, to another gifts of healings by the same Spirit, to another the working of miracles, to another prophecy, to another discerning of spirits, to another different kinds of tongues, to another the interpretation of tongues. But one and the same Spirit works all these things, distributing to each one individually as He wills.*

The Holy Spirit is also the driving force behind every great revival as He refreshes and restores God's people. Consider the Azusa Street Revival that went on for three years and the Fulton Street Revival that reported over one million souls saved.

Young prophet do not be seduced by the spirit of this age, which wants you to believe the ministry of the Holy Spirit is passé. It encourages new churchgoers that the fervent expression of His presence is emotionalism. Furthermore, it teaches you that God is more concerned with your initial acceptance of Him then He is about how you walk out your eternal soul's salvation (Philippians 2:12). I am not minimizing the salvation experience; however, it is just as important that we teach people not to stop there. If an individual never goes past his initial encounter, he does not possess any power to effect change or advance the kingdom of God.

Prophet of God you cannot be trepid in releasing the ministry of His power in every atmosphere where God has given you jurisdiction. Paul urged Timothy in 2 Timothy 1:6-7 (AMP),

> *That is why I remind you to fan into flame the gracious gift of God, [that inner fire—the special endowment] which is in you through the laying on of my hands [with those of the elders at your ordination]. For God did not give us a spirit of timidity or cowardice or fear, but [He has given us a spirit] of power and of love and of sound judgment and personal discipline [abilities that result in a calm, well-balanced mind and self-control].*

Many today make new believers fearful of the Holy Spirit rather than embrace His ministry. They must be taught that He is not to be judged by a church's liturgical style but by the work He does that is in alignment with the scriptures.

8

THE SPIRIT-FILLED CHURCH

When I minister as a prophet, I understand that it is not important that I touch the people; rather, it is far more important that they have a bona fide encounter with the Holy Spirit. A. W. Tozer said:

If the Holy Spirit was withdrawn from the church today, 95 percent of what we do would go on, and no one would know the difference. If the Holy Spirit had been withdrawn from the New Testament church, 95 percent of what they did would stop, and everybody would know the difference.

The church without the Holy Spirit is not the church; for in the Holy Spirit, the church *"lives and moves and has our being"* (Acts 17:28). The church today struggles with understanding who the Holy Spirit is and what His function is in the church. Scripture confirms that He is the successor of Jesus in God's redemptive plan (John 14:16, 17).

It's disheartening that we sacrifice spiritual power for innovation. The church's mantra today is, "Lights! Camera! Action!" Today's Christians go to church week after week and never have a spiritual encounter. They rush to the altar and are never truly converted. Often, what we call the Holy Spirit is mere emotionalism, church liturgy and a spirit of religion. That is why many come out of the church unchanged and perpetually impotent. The Christian walk today is void and empty. We live life on the fence, no conviction, no holiness, no power, no inspiration, no sanctification, desiring to see exactly how close we can pitch our tents to Sodom (Genesis 13:12).

Because Jesus knew His disciples would forge the church ahead, He commanded them to wait until they were filled with power. John 20:21, 22: *"So Jesus said to them again, 'Peace to you! As the Father has sent Me, I also send you.' And when He had said this, He breathed on them, and said to them, 'Receive the Holy Spirit.'"* The church's understanding of how powerful the Holy Spirit is in their lives is up to them. When you are filled, you cannot get unfilled; you can only grieve the Holy Spirit

> *Let no corrupt word proceed out of your mouth, but what is good for necessary edification, that it may impart grace to the hearers. And do not grieve the Holy Spirit of God…Let all bitterness, wrath, anger, clamor and evil speaking be put away from you…be kind to one another, tenderhearted, forgiving one another, even as God in Christ forgave you* (Ephesians 4:29-32).

Full maturity in the Holy Spirit is the manifestation of the fruit of the Spirit operating at maximum capacity in a church or a believer.

9

PROPHET NOT FOR PROFIT

Sowing money into a prophet's ministry is scriptural, and it is one of the ways God prospers His people. The distressed widow gave Elisha her last jar of oil. 2 Kings 4:7 says, *"Then she came and told the man of God. And he said, "Go, sell the oil and pay your debt; and you and your sons live on the rest."* As she followed the prophet's instructions, God multiplied her resources.

Before going to battle in the wilderness of Tekoa, King Jehoshaphat urged the people to rely on the validity of the prophet's message and leading. He promised them that if they believed the prophet Jahaziel, they would prosper. 2 Chronicles 20:20 says, *"Jehoshaphat stood and said, hear me, O Judah, and ye inhabitants of Jerusalem; Believe in the LORD your God, so shall ye be established; believe his prophets, so shall ye prosper."*

Paul wrote to the Corinthians, *"In the same way, the Lord has commanded that those who preach the gospel should receive their living from the gospel"* (1 Corinthians 9:14, NIV), but we are not to take advantage. In response to Elisha's ministry, Naaman offered him a gift. Elisha's response in 2 Kings 5:16 (NIV) was, *"As surely as the LORD lives, whom I serve, I will not accept a thing."* Although giving to a prophet is in order, it is crucial to remember no monetary value can be placed on a word from the Lord. Prophecies are not for sale! Experientially, I understand that the more visible you are, the higher the compensation but compensation must not lead to compromise. The power God has given a prophet to release prosperity and provision can easily turn into covetousness if the prophet is not careful.

For clarification, the Greek word for prosper is *euodoó,*[9] which means, "properly, to go on a prosperous journey." Therefore, prosperity is not only related to a person's financial condition (3 John 1:2). The prosperity of the soul is the predominant need. If people get healed in their emotions, God can teach them how to prosper financially.

PRACTICAL PROPHETIC LIVING

The prophet who follows Jesus must be completely devoted to Him. The quest for money and worldly pleasures creates divided loyalties. Money is an inanimate object; therefore, it cannot be good or evil. The nature of money is determined by the hand that holds it. The love of money opens the door to lust (1 Timothy 6:10). In Matthew 6, Jesus is ministering to the multitudes regarding the spiritual disciplines of this new order of worship. They were no longer bound by the Ten Commandments but the condition of their hearts. He talked to them about fasting, prayer, charitable deeds and the dangers of wealth.

In Matthew 6:24 (NKJV), Jesus declares to them, *"No one can serve two masters; for either he will hate the one and love the other, or else he will be loyal to the one and despise the other. You cannot serve God and mammon."* Mammon is "the idolatrous worship of riches, money, possessions and/or property." The word, in the biblical text, comes from the Greek word *mammōnás*,[10] a Semitic term for "the treasure a person trusts in." The heart of a prophet will be tested.

I receive honorariums one of two ways: first through love offerings with no set fee, and secondly, through a set fee determined by the church. A set fee compensation is usually determined by the size of the meeting. I also request a vendor table to make my books and products available for purchase. It is my practice when I minister to stay in the confines of the church's budget. I will not ask for a large amount of money if only ten people are in attendance. If you do not have drawing power, you do not have the right to demand exorbitant fees. Making a divine deposit is far more important to me than being paid because I understand that God provides for me—not men.

It is important that a prophet recognizes honorariums are a privilege—not a right. People bless us because they understand that we need to earn a living and they appreciate and honor the ministry. However, the prophets in the Bible were taken care of by God, and He moved on men to provide for them. Putting strict requirements on what we need to show up is absurd. Simply go, and God will make provision. Moreover, I am not endorsing that we go for free either because ministry cost money. I am also aware of the fact that there are so many churches that will take advantage of God's prophets. They want for free what it cost you to produce.

PRACTICAL PROPHETIC LIVING

I am an itinerate prophet in Oklahoma and have been ministering there for over a decade. For the first few years, I paid my way. One year, the pastor decided to sow into my life and provision has been made for me ever since. After ministering, in a service, the pastor implored his congregation to sow a seed into my life as they felt led of the Lord. I stood there with my daughters and began to weep. People sowed into my life for nearly thirty minutes. What their sowing told me was how much they honored my service and dedication—not only to them but the Lord. You cannot demand honor—you earn it.

Honorariums are not my sole provision. One of my favorite scriptures is in Proverbs 8:12, which says, *"I wisdom dwell with prudence, and find out knowledge of witty inventions" (KJV)*. God has given me several inventions, books, and business strategies to support the ministry; Paul was a tentmaker (Acts 18:3). God's directive to me was, "Stop giving away for free what I gave you to prosper." On the other hand, I believe that God is raising up a new breed of prophets that will not have to sell what we *should* be giving away for free. I decree that this new breed of prophets is fiscally responsible and astute.

Finally, a prophet not for profit will protect the sheep. A prophet for profit will fleece them and leave them open for attack. Thus, your primary responsibility is to protect the sheep and feed them, not financially rape them.

10

THE SIN OF DUPLICATION

In his book, *The Anointing: Yesterday, Today and Tomorrow*, R. T. Kendall said he was following his normal devotional routine when one morning, he read 1 Samuel 16:1 and the verse literally leaped out at him.

> *Now the LORD said to Samuel, "How long will you mourn for Saul, seeing I have rejected him from reigning over Israel? Fill your horn with oil, and go; I am sending you to Jesse the Bethlehemite. For I have provided Myself a king among his sons.*

Kendall said, "In a flash, I saw three eras: yesterday's man (King Saul), today's man (Samuel) and tomorrow's man (David)." Bishop Joseph Garlington said of *The Anointing*, "Every man who leads and every leader who follows should read this book on their knees."

R. T. Kendal's insight showed me how many people and churches desire to build their ministry after an old pattern. They spend money and resources trying to mimic what God did for someone else, but God is in the "fresh-oil" business. What worked for one church or ministry may not work for another.

Have the courage to chart new territory and make new paths. Ministry formats and programs are implemented without ever seeking God about what He wants. Ministry leaders want so desperately to recapture the anointing of an old movement. I was listening to a well-known prophetic evangelist as he discussed his recent ministry itinerary. For one of the events, he said, "There was an incredible movement going on in that city." For the other event, he said, "He needed to return because there was a tremendous outpouring."

There is a difference between a movement and an outpouring. A movement will eventually die, but an outpouring will go on for years and transcend generations. Elijah's life was an outpouring. 2 Kings 13:21 says, *"So it was, as they were burying a man, that suddenly they spied a band of raiders; and they put the man in the tomb of Elisha; and when the man was let down and touched the bones of Elisha, he revived and stood on his feet."*

Lastly, I was reading the book, *The Secret of His Power* about Smith Wigglesworth, and I could feel the power of the Holy Spirit flow through the pages as I read the book. Prophet of God, as you dig new wells, don't let your ministry die with you and do not try to duplicate what is already in the earth. Generations to come should hear about the work you did, the ground you plowed and the miracles you wrought. They should read about what you did and be revived. Daniel 11:32 says, *"Those who do wickedly against the covenant he shall corrupt with flattery, but the people who know their God shall be strong, and carry out great exploits."*

11

WHOLE AND HOLY

The word "integrity" comes from the Latin word *integritatem,*[11] from which come the English words "integration" and "integer." It implies "soundness, wholeness, and completeness." Purity is a byproduct of being whole. Remaining authentic when you still have open wounds that require feeding is quite difficult. If you have breaches in your soul, you will always need something outside of yourself to make you feel complete. Psalm 107:9 (KJV) says, *"For he satisfieth the longing soul, and filleth the hungry soul with goodness."* The culmination of integrity is emotional and spiritual integration.

The scriptures remind us that our fleshly nature is never satisfied (Proverbs 27:20). The woman at the well was on a constant quest to satisfy her aching soul. Because of her lack of integrity, five husbands and a boyfriend later, she was still searching (John 4:18). She did not become whole until her encounter with Jesus ended her emotional drought and halted her fleshly pursuits (John 4:14).

As a prophet, you must be comfortable with God's molding and shaping while He is making you whole. He is the potter, and you are the clay (Isaiah 64:8). These periods are times of surgical intervention to rid the prophet of lingering emotional baggage, healing the wounds from the previous season and preparing them for the next. If you do not understand this, you will try to cram the empty space with people and things while ignoring the lessons learned.

I must admit that during these seasons, God can feel extremely distant. I have had to remind myself that part of the strength of my ministry is wholeness and holiness. You must learn to live life in the valley, not on the mountaintop. A prophet's ministry is characterized by atmospheres that are supercharged with Holy-Ghost fire, and it is very difficult sometimes to live your life in between those moments.

During these seasons staying on the potter's wheel and keeping your divine assignment in plain view is so important, simply because veering off the path and embracing something that brings relief and seems more exciting and fulfilling can be easy. You feel alive and fulfilled when you are operating in your anointing but many times, you are frustrated and disillusioned when the "glory cloud" lifts, and the surgeon is sharpening his scalpel.

More times than not, when people hear the word "prophet," they simultaneously think false. Therefore, for you, emerging prophets, integrity and character should be your primary pursuit. The gift and ministry will take care of itself. The instruction that was given to me long before I even understood the gift or knew I had it was that the life of God's prophet is hard. Learn how to yield to the call.

Integrity in prophetic ministry is so vital because we should be beacons of light and hope. We cannot bring anyone into a holy relationship with God if our relationship with Him is fractured. David, a man after God's own heart, led God's people with integrity first and gifting second (Psalm 78:72). Stay on the potter's wheel and make it your assignment to bring HONOR back to the office of the prophet.

12

PROPHETIC SEASONS

As previously addressed, transitioning well and being in between seasons and assignments can be very difficult for a prophet. After Elijah conquered the prophets of Baal, he fell into a deep depression. You are most vulnerable after a great victory. The prophetic life is a series of transitions, so it is important to know what season you are in. You must be clear on the instruction that God has given you to help sustain you in this season.

In transition, you are not gaining ground. Rather, you are being anchored deeper into your purpose and waiting for your next assignment. This seeming delay is not the time to be anxious or impatient; take inventory and stock of where you are in God. *"Examine yourselves as to whether you are in the faith"* (2 Corinthians 13:5). *Inventory* means "to make a complete list of what is in place, removing what is not beneficial and acquiring what is." Prophets who fail to take inventory can subject themselves to unnecessary attacks.

One year, I took a sabbatical, and I discovered that leave of absence was one of the most crucial moves I have ever made. Failure to obey the prompting of the Holy Spirit would have left me mired in a pit of doing church work and ignoring my prophetic mantle for the sake of comfort. Church service is noble and good if it is what God is telling you to do; however, we cannot use church service instead of obedience. Talking *about* God is not talking *to* Him; serving Him is *not* always obeying Him.

Learning to transition from one season to another effectively was an art and took much discipline and prayer. At one time in my life when I felt like I was not advancing, I simply asked the Holy Spirit, "What is hindering me?" With an eager heart to hear and positioned to make the changes, I heard Him say, "You are too impulsive."

Hearing those words was paramount as I realized that sometimes during the difficult seasons, I can be too eager to lean toward what is habitual to get relief, rather than travel unfamiliar terrain. Since a prophet's ministry needs to be very strategic, his being overly impulsive can be disastrous.

Impulsivity is "moving too fast without getting information or confirmation from the Holy Spirit." It's doing what we think is good but may not be right! It can open the door to unnecessary entanglements. It can be what the scriptures call a besetting sin. Hebrews 12:1 (KJV) says, "*Wherefore seeing we also are compassed about with so great a cloud of witnesses, let us lay aside every weight, and the sin which doth so easily beset [us], and let us run with patience the race that is set before us.*"

The Greek translation of the word "beset" is *euperistatos*,[12] which means, "to encircle or be easily distracted and (figuratively) a serious hindrance that 'encircles' (hampers) someone who desperately needs to advance." Some common examples include giving more of our time and resources than God requires without counting the impact on our families or ministries. Secondly, eating without considering the effect it has on our health or making commitments without considering the impact on our already crammed calendar. The most common impulse for a prophet is being drawn to the broken or those who are in distress. We can waste a lot of time ministering to people who have no ambition or motivation to change.

In your current state, this behavior can have minimal impact. However, the effects can be disastrous where you are going. Being too impulsive can lead to sin and activate a sin cycle that can take years to end or get under control. Everything good is not God. You can be doing good down the wide road of destruction. The sins that hurt us the most are not the big ones but the "little foxes" (Song of Solomon 2:15)! *Sin* is "anything that is done without the express permission of the Holy Spirit through the Word or direction and ultimately separates us from God. I encourage you to take inventory today!

The environment is everything. Keep yourself in an environment that forces change and puts a demand on your anointing. Your advancement and success in God are assured! No matter what kind of transition you are involved in presently, stepping into your new season takes time, patience, and preparation. Because the prophetic office takes so long to train, slow and steady is the preferred method. Of course, you can forge ahead without God, but nothing born of the flesh will ever become spirit; changing the hands on the clock to suit you doesn't change the time.

PRACTICAL PROPHETIC LIVING

13

THE JEZEBEL FACTOR

Jezebel was relentless in her pursuit of Elijah because he was the only one who could oppose and rival her authority. We often hear about Christians coming against this vicious spirit but based on biblical accounts Jezebel's focus was destroying the prophets of God. This spirit will always follow prophetic people because the prophetic gift frustrates the plans of a manipulative and religious spirit.

Furthermore, the spirit of witchcraft has become synonymous with Jezebel. Because Jezebel was Ahab's wife, she could only operate through delegated authority and had no authority of her own. In its simplest form, *witchcraft* is "someone using illegal authority to get what they want and advance their wicked plans at the expense of others." Because the spirit of Jezebel is always looking for areas of weakness that it can capitalize on, it skillfully watches its victim. The spirit's defining characteristic is its ability to immobilize its prey by fear and intimidation. It is a very aggressive spirit that comes to hijack the prophetic anointing.

1 Kings 18:19 records that Jezebel, Ahab's wife, had a consortium of 850 false prophets eating at her table. She provided for 450 prophets of Baal, the storm god, and 400 prophets of Asherah, who was known as the goddess of heaven. She consorted with false prophets but slaughtered and massacred the prophets of God (1 Kings 18:4). She despised Elijah and utilized every tactic she could to silence him and render him ineffective. She only wanted prophets who would say what she wanted to hear and support her evil agenda. The spirit of Jezebel is always trying to kill the prophets, but at the word of Elisha and by the sword of Jehu, God avenged the prophets and is still avenging them today (2 Kings 9:1-7).

In the modern-day church, people who are driven by this spirit always try to gain positions of power by developing close relationships with those in authority, i.e., the pastor and the pastor's wife. They present themselves as being very nice, knowledgeable, educated, and helpful, which can make them very difficult to detect. What the spirit is trying to do is infiltrate the organization and identify areas of weakness, so it can bring destruction and division. As a pastor of a church, it is important to have seasoned, trained, and trusted prophets in your ministry. Their function is to help neutralize this spirit's assault because a prophet of God has the responsibility to protect God's church.

The Prophet and Rebellion

I Samuel 15:23 says, *"For rebellion is as the sin of witchcraft, and stubbornness is as iniquity and idolatry."* Rebellion is listed as the moral equivalent of witchcraft. An immature prophet has the proclivity to lean towards this type of behavior. Because of this weakness repentance can sometimes be extremely difficult. Unconfessed sin can lead to pride and pride can open the door to a stubborn spirit, this can be crippling for a prophet. When a prophet disobeys God or sins against Him or His people the consequences are steep.

Consider the account of the prophet whom God told not to eat with anyone in the city. He told him to speak to the altar and leave (1 Kings 13:1-24). Because the prophet disobeyed God, the lions killed him and left his dead carcass to rot. Moses was a great prophet of God, but because of disobedience and a bad temper, he was not able to enter the Promised Land (Numbers 20).

When in leadership, the prophet must be careful not to allow the spirit of Jezebel to control the people to build their ministry. Once service and church attendance are excessively demanded, it becomes manipulation. Prophets are not in the controlling business but in the soul-building business and volunteerism is a mechanism used to teach people to serve God—not the leader. The spirit of witchcraft castrates the church and makes it impotent. The church ends up with a group of under developed prophets who look to the leader for guidance, rather than God.

When disobedience festers, a prophet can almost, if he is not careful, become uncorrectable. If a prophet is not careful, his gift can become a weapon of mass destruction. Prophets can become master manipulators to continue experiencing the life their gifts garnered for them. Their continued manipulation will cripple people, rather than heal them.

Additionally, a prophet must also remember that the scripture says that God's gifts are without repentance; therefore, a disobedient prophet can continue to prophesy although God's presence has been lifted from him (Romans 11:29). When a prophet can no longer hear God's voice or sense His presence, he will start seeking the counsel of familiar spirits or start prophesying out of the soulish realm.

The penalty of sin and disobedience will always be a high price to pay. Jesus paid a tremendous price for our sins, so let us remain free. Galatians 5:1 says, *"Stand fast therefore in the liberty by which Christ has made us free, and do not be entangled again with a yoke of bondage."*

The Prophet and Sexual Immorality

A prophet must be vigilant about not allowing feelings of abandonment and alienation open the door to sexual sins. The Bible commands believers to flee from sexual immorality. We are admonished in I Corinthians 6:18 (AMP),

> *Run away from sexual immorality [in any form, whether thought or behavior, whether visual or written]. Every other sin that a man commits is outside the body, but the one who is sexually immoral sins against his own body.*

Sexual immorality can manifest in a person's life in various ways. The behavior expresses itself through pornography, masturbation, bestiality, fornication, homosexuality, and adultery. If a prophet is not careful, he can use illicit sex to feel emotionally connected. A professional psychologist told me, "Sexual sins are about intimacy, not sex." However, it is still a sin that God hates. Ephesians 5:3 (AMP) says,

> *But sexual immorality and all [moral] impurity [indecent, offensive behavior] or greed must not even be hinted at among you, as is proper*

among saints [for as believers our way of life, whether in public or in private, reflects the validity of our faith].

For prophetic people, sexual sin is a dangerous trap and a vicious snare. Like any other sins, sexual promiscuity and perversion are forgivable but deadly. Unless we repent, the penalty we must pay can destroy an entire ministry. Jesus refers to this sin as *"the depths of Satan"* (Revelations 2:22-24).

It is purely satanic and is a means by which demonic spirits can swiftly transfer from one person to another. A pastor gives an account of a woman he was counseling. During the counseling session, the woman was moving in and out of different personalities. The pastor said the Holy Spirit told him, "She does not need counseling; she needs hands laid on her. Those personalities are the manifestation of every man she ever slept with."

My physical and emotional brokenness culminated in a life of fornication and adultery. It is the one sin that kept me on my knees. I struggled so much in this area and desperately wanted deliverance. I did not understand, at that time, when we have sexual intercourse outside of marriage, we fuse ourselves to another person, and those ties need to be broken.

The other thing that contributed to my lascivious lifestyle was being molested at the age of thirteen. The man who molested me was heavily involved in pornography. He had a shed full of *Playboy, Hustler,* and every lewd magazine in publication at that time. The moment he touched me, I felt immediately dirty, and it opened the door to an addiction to pornography in my teenage years. That molestation opened the door to desires that I was too immature to handle and consequently carried me down a path that took me years to break. Because of God's goodness and my obedience, I can say today; I am free!

Lacking discipline or not being healed in this area will destroy a prophet's ministry. It invalidates him in the eyes of people who will indefinitely question his authenticity and integrity. People are looking for a prophet who can keep the standard raised as well as someone they can look up to and follow. Prophets must remain vigilant over their ministry and solicit the help of the Holy Spirit to remain pure. I admit that it is difficult to stay celibate if you have already opened the door to sexual pleasure, but it is not impossible. By her admission, the woman who led me to the Lord was very promiscuous before she accepted Christ. After she got saved, she asked God to make her a virgin again. For over ten years, she remained abstinent until she eventually got married.

Another reason sexual purity is a must in the prophetic ministry that because many flow in the gift of healing and impartation, which often operates through the laying on of hands (Acts 28:8). As discussed, the human touch is a means of transference; you impart who you are—not what you believe or teach. Our mission is to release liberty into the souls of people, not bondage.

The Penalty for Sexual Immorality

The church of Thyatira was known to be a community where God was worshiped. Lydia, who was a seller of purple in Thyatira, was a member of this church (Acts 16:14). Lydia loved God, and He opened her heart, so she could obey the truths that Paul the apostle was teaching (Acts 16:14). Jesus even encouraged and commended the church of Thyatira in Revelation 2:19, which says, *"I know your works, love, service, faith and your patience; and as for your works, the last are more than the first."*

Even though the members were patient, lovers of God, and served well, they were known as the corrupt church. As a prophet, you can have all your spiritual disciplines in place but still be corrupt. The word "corrupt" comes from the Greek word *phthora*,[13] which means "rottenness, decay, and destruction, which has to do with an *internal flaw*." Why would Jesus call a church that loved Him so much, corrupt?

In Revelation 2:20, He said, *"Nevertheless, I have a few things against you, because you allow that woman Jezebel, who calls herself a prophetess, to teach and seduce My servants to commit sexual immorality."* Underneath the people's excellent church service, they were perverse.

We know from 2 Kings 9:30-37 that Jezebel was killed; her flesh was eaten, and her blood lapped up by the dogs. So, we can deduce in the above passage that *Jezebel* is now a spirit that inhabits a person. Now, we see the spirit manifesting itself through the gay agenda because one of its assignments is to castrate men and violate God's commandment to be fruitful and multiply. A new breed of churches is arising with the pastors' titles being "Pastor and First Gentlemen or Husband." The truth is that spirit hates the church and only wants to corrupt it. One of the roots of homosexuality is rebellion, hating order, rules, regulations, and authority. The homosexual agenda is deception packaged in the truth that "God is love." You also see this spirit attaching itself to Hollywood because it wants to control the media and hypnotize a new generation. The spirit of Jezebel wants people to accept this vile lifestyle as *normal*. The *Homosexual Manifesto* published in 1987, by gay revolutionary Michael Swift, is this spirit's evil agenda and plan for our sons.

According to Revelation 2:22-23 the penalty for sexual sins is infirmity, great distress, and misery; Jesus Himself will cut off the posterity of the person who embraces these sins. In the practical sense, our children suffer when we live a life of sexual immorality. The reward for those who do not adhere to this philosophy is spiritual authority. Sexual immorality is directly related to a person's prophetic power, authority, and ability to rule.

14

PROPHETIC INCUBATION

Prophet Kris Vallotton wrote, "It takes about 15 years to train a prophet." The validity of that statement was also expressed in my training. I spent exactly 15 years in the prophetic house to which God sent me. I spent most of my service in the music ministry and at the altar praying for people.

In the music ministry, I learned two crucial lessons that helped solidify my prophetic call. I learned how to cultivate the Holy Spirit's presence because Kris Valloton said, "The anointing ebbs and flows based on how much time you spend with Him." That is the reason why you can hear some prophets speak, and you can hardly maintain your composure. However, with others, you cannot wait for the message to end. These messages contain too much flesh because the prophet has not spent enough time with the Holy Spirit. The other lesson God taught me was that He would not allow me to live by the approval of man.

The time I spent in this ministry was difficult as well as rewarding. Every encounter with God was new and fresh, but I also did not understand what God was doing in my life. He constantly showed me things in dreams and visions, so I began to write what I heard and what I saw. This very book was birthed out of those days of living life in a crucible of affliction. However, this time created so much confusion because I was not comfortable interacting with God in this dimension. In retrospect, I realize He was training me for the office in which I would later stand.

A biblical account regarding John the Baptist is given in Luke 1:80, which says, *"So the child grew and became strong in spirit, and was in the deserts till the day of his manifestation to Israel."* Also, those silent years, as in the life of John the Baptist, were times of training so that the prophet would be fully equipped for his ministry. Some information is given about his birth in Luke 1:36, and his next appearance was in Matthew 3 as a voice crying in the wilderness: *"Prepare the way of the LORD"* (3:4). Do not be too anxious about ministry; God's timing is perfect. He knows exactly when you are ready for your assignment and He has an incredible way of setting the stage for your arrival.

Elijah simply appeared on the scene. Not much is known about him other than he was a Tishbite from Gilead. God was preparing his prophetic entrance. Because little is understood about the timing of God, Ahab and Jezebel had to be at the height of their tyranny before Elijah could even show up. As Ahab was erecting altars for Baal and worshipping false gods (1 Kings 16:33-35), God was preparing Elijah to confront the spiritual, religious and political alliance that Ahab the King made with his father-in-law Ethbaal, king of the Zidonians

I suspect that between 1 Kings 16:35 and 1 Kings 17:1, God was speaking to Elijah and fortifying him for the coming challenge. Baal was known as the storm god, so Elijah's assignment was to prove to the people that God alone controlled the elements. Elijah declared in 1 Kings 17:1, *"There shall not be dew nor rain these years."* Packed in Elijah's assignment was prophetic provision and protection. God told Elijah to hide by the Brook Cherith where the Ravens would feed him at His command. For Elijah's protection, he was divinely hidden so that he was positioned to finish his assignment. Ahab had extensively searched the land and adjacent countries but was unable to locate Elijah (1 Kings 18:10). As Obadiah, Ahab's treasurer, stated in 1 Kings 18:12 (NET), *"But when I leave you, the LORD's spirit will carry you away so I can't find you."* Obviously, God intentionally protected Elijah.

God has a plan, and He is patient to make sure every detail is in place before He releases you to enter your arena. He wants to make sure you are ready and equipped to complete the assignment ahead. So many prophets enter the arena prematurely. Unfortunately, they do not last long, or they self-destruct. Sadly, they never complete their assignments. I Timothy 3:5-7 (AMP) says,

> *For if a man does not know how to manage his own household, how will he take care of the church of God?). and He must not be a new convert, so that he will not [behave stupidly and] become conceited [by appointment to this high office] and fall into the [same] condemnation incurred by the devil [for his arrogance and pride]. And he must have a good*

reputation and be well thought of by those outside the church, so that he will not be discredited and fall into the devil's trap.

The most important qualities that a prophet must possess are patience and trust. He must patiently await God's plan and trust that God knows what He is doing. God told Jeremiah, *"For **I know** the plans I have for you," declares the* LORD, *"plans to prosper you and not to harm you, plans to give you hope and a future"* (Jeremiah 29:11, NIV).

15

OF MANTLE AND OF MEN

Inherent in a prophetic mantle is the spiritual authority that is passed down from one prophet to another. Although the prophet may die, the God of the prophet still lives. I heard a Pastor say, "Mantles and anointings do not leave the earthly realm; they must be reassigned. If no one qualifies, then it will lay dormant in the earth until the next qualified person picks it up."

Look at the life of the healing evangelist, Katherine Kuhlman. When she left, her healing mantle was transferred to Benny Hinn. He positioned himself to qualify for it by seeking the counsel of the Holy Spirit through fasting and prayer. Benny Hinn even expressed that while Katherine Kuhlman was in the hospital dying, he tried to see her but was never able to make the connection. He said, "God told me that if I had met her, I would have thought she gave me something." God alone is the keeper of the mantle—not a person.

The story of Elijah and Elisha is the most popular story in relationship to the prophetic mantle. Elisha was destined to pick up Elijah's mantle (1 Kings 19:19). Based on their story, we ascertain that resident in the mantle is the kingdom authority to fulfill the office because the Bible says that Elisha performed twice as many miracles as did Elijah.

Another biblical account of Elijah's mantle is demonstrated in the life of John the Baptist's (Luke 1:15-18). The scripture says he wore a cloak of fur and girded around his waist was a thick leather belt. Obviously, the prophets were distinguishable by their garments, which were symbolic of a life of sacrifice—not indulgence. Unfortunately, a new breed of prophets has entered the scene who believe that it is important to wear the finest clothes, imported shoes, and silk ties. My understanding, which is based on Scripture, is that a prophet was modest in his appearance and did not give much credence to what he looked like on the outside.

As mentioned previously, spiritual mantles are not relegated to time; the practice was here long before we came and will be here long after we are gone. The Lord spoke to me one day and said, "There are no new messages in the earth. What exists is someone being sensitive enough to pick up the mantle from the previous generation."

One of my dearest prophetic friends operates under the healing mantle of John G. Lake. I was in a service while he was ministering in the prophetic, and the presence of God was so concentrated, it felt like time was standing still. As the prophet began to speak, I heard the Holy Spirit confirm this.

The mantle can be the same, but there will be differences in the way it operates with one's specific personality. Prophetically, we don't start anything new; we take up where the mantle left off. In the next generation, God gives you a man's anointing to do the same thing in a greater capacity.

Very few prophets seem to have a succession plan. During my ministry, the Lord spoke to me about three young ladies with whom I was supposed to pour my spirit and make them mantle-ready. I have spent countless hours with these young ladies doing life with them—helping them rear children, teaching them the principles of prophetic living, ministering to them about marriage and everything that would help them live successfully. I find it interesting that God chose three young ladies because I have three natural daughters into whom I have poured my spirit as well. I believe because of my faithfulness God is now sending others. My spiritual duty and obligation are to make sure that my ministry does not die with me, leaving my mantle to lay dormant for a generation. As leaders, our succession plan must be thoroughly and strategically thought out.

Prophets must be dedicated to rear sons and daughters so that the generation after us will have the opportunity to experience God the way we did. I read John Bevere's book entitled *Honor's Reward: How to Attract God's Favor and Blessing*, and realized it is important to understand that the transference of prophetic mantles is orchestrated through honor and respect. We cannot follow someone we do not respect, let alone receive an impartation from him.

Lastly, we are now seeing a trend in ministry where fathers or mothers are passing the ministry mantle to their children. Just because someone is related to you does not mean they qualify to carry the mantle. On the contrary, there are mantles assigned to specific families. For example, Moses' elder brother Aaron and his sons all walked in the priesthood.

The Holy Spirit showed me if a mantle is not picked up in the next generation the demonic spirit defeated by the mantle, in the previous generation, can assault the family lineage. Recently, I was teaching a class on healing and three women in the class, who were related, were all bound by a spirit of infirmity. As I spoke to one of the women after the class, they shared with me their grandfather was a healing evangelist who ministered to thousands. I believe because no one picked up the mantle of healing the spirit of infirmity could roam unopposed throughout the blood-line.

A prophet by the name of Steve Thompson once said, "Our predecessor's ceiling has become our floor." Roberts Liardon, the author of *God's Generals: Why They Succeeded and Why Some Failed*, also said, "You are the sum of everyone who has imparted into you." Prophet pick up your mantle!

16

MANTLE READY

"Everywhere in Christendom, we see the divine system cluttered with the tawdry trappings of flesh, the flawless luster of divine revelation desecrated with human fingerprints." – Unknown

It was the summer of 1993 at the Azusa Conference in Tulsa, Oklahoma. I had spent years seeking God, praying, fasting and asking Him for more. I had never heard of the term "prophetic mantle" and did not realize I was making myself mantle ready. I simply knew there was more, and I was hungry for it. One morning, during the conference at the Mabee Center, with strategic interruption, Oral Roberts bellowed a prophetic utterance regarding the significance of the Azusa Street Revival, the changing of the guard, and the closing of the ages.

Now, he was prophesying that 87 or so years later, another would come and unleash a fresh wind in the power of the Holy Spirit. I, without coincidence, was present and accounted for at that meeting as the atmosphere was charged with a prophetic assignment. I remember my former pastor was being introduced, and it would be the first time our lives intersected. His church would be the place where I would spend the next 15 years. I had no idea that I was about to be enrolled in prophet school.

The closing of the ages would be the destruction of the bondages enforced by religion, and people would worship in the liberty of the Spirit. The apostle Paul wrote not of the letter, but of the Spirit. *"For the letter kills, but the Spirit gives life"* (2 Corinthians 3:6). God knew what was on the horizon, and a prophetic tapestry was being woven.

The lead article in the conference magazine entitled "Of Mantle and of Men" was penned by my former pastor. The words that rang in my spirit like the Liberty Bell were "The mantle is now falling" I knew something in me quickened, and I had to get there—wherever there was. I began a frantic search to find out where the mantle was falling! The moment I stepped over the threshold of the church, I knew that I had entered more than a religious edifice but a strategic posturing of the kingdom of God in the earth.

What transpired was not a mere inception of a church, but a historical event that must be chronicled in the annals of history and not lost—a modern-day Azusa Street Revival. People drove, flew, had visions, and heard the directive of the Holy Spirit to come. They traveled thousands of miles to get fresh water. The prophet declared, "This church will more than double in the next year." Indeed, the church grew from 300 or so to an explosion of over 10,000. It was so reminiscent of the accounts of the Azusa Street Revival where people would step on American soil, be slain by the power of the Holy Spirit and be eternally changed.

Countless people were healed and filled with the Holy Spirit, and my ten-year-old daughter was one of them. There were no boundaries; the clarion call had been made regardless of age, creed or color. It was a true gathering and equipping of the prophets; a mantle was released. The prophetic anointing had not been demonstrated in that magnitude (to my knowledge) in many years. The prophets gathered from miles around without a marketing extravaganza, social media, television or radio. It was merely the voice of the Lord that had gathered the people. A company of prophets with a healing anointing were in the birth canal.

Week after week, the word of the Lord that would fracture and sever religious factions was catapulted in power across the pulpit. It was etched in our spirits like ink on paper. I was like a sponge absorbing every word. The word of the Lord was delivered in a way that few have the privilege to experience. The power of the Holy Spirit was once again awakened. The church was a fragrant incense being released into the atmosphere. The mulberry tree was once again rustling with the sound.

The mantle that fell will transcend many generations. I have many times shared with my children how privileged we were to be a part of what God was doing in the earth. There are many stories; mine is only one. Full circle for me is that one of my daughters is attending Oral Roberts University. We now know how significant it all was and how all our lives were supernaturally interwoven. We count it an honor to have been present. Twenty-three years later, the prophet is gathering the next generation of prophets and preparing them to carry the mantle in their generation.

As with any large church or movement, conflict will arise. Many wanted the prophet to do more, and critics were looming at every corner. However, stewarding a move that you didn't even realize you were in is extremely difficult. Only in retrospect can you now see divine footprints. The man of God's assignment was to release the mantle, and if you were there when he went up, you could have it!

PRACTICAL PROPHETIC LIVING

17

THE SPIRIT OF GAHAZI

One of our ministry assignments is to raise up prophets who are not for profit. The prophetic ministry can garner an individual great wealth and resources, but gifts and trinkets must be accepted only with God's approval. At the word of Elisha, Naaman was healed from a life of leprosy. A natural response was to give an offering. The prophet Elisha adamantly refused his gift. 2 Kings 5:15-16 says,

> *And he returned to the man of God, he and all his aides, and came and stood before him; and he said, "Indeed, now I know that there is no God in all the earth, except in Israel; now, therefore, please take a gift from your servant." But he said, "As the Lord lives, before whom I stand, I will receive nothing." And he urged him to take it, but he refused.*

Elijah's servant Gehazi thought he would capitalize on Elisha's refusal. 2 Kings 5:25-27 (NIV) documents Elisha's response to Gehazi's treachery.

> *When he went in and stood before his master, Elisha asked him, "Where have you been, Gehazi?"*

> *"Your servant didn't go anywhere," Gehazi answered.*

> *But Elisha said to him, "Was not my spirit with you when the man got down from his chariot to meet you? Is this the time to take money or to accept clothes—or olive groves and vineyards, or flocks and herds, or male and female slaves? Naaman's leprosy will cling to you and to your descendants forever." Then Gehazi went from Elisha's presence, and his skin was leprous—it had become as white as snow.*

Three lessons can be ascertained from this biblical account. Initially, a prophet must rely only on God's provision. Everything is not for financial gain, and if we make every ministry encounter an opportunity to profit, it no longer becomes a blessing from the Lord. Rather, the encounter becomes a lust for filthy lucre.

Secondly, be careful to ask the Holy Spirit to search the motives of those around you. So many people will want to attach themselves to you simply to profit from your anointing, obedience, and ministry.

Thirdly, Elisha was a prophet with integrity. No one would have even questioned if he had accepted the gifts from Naaman, but he knew that God alone needed to be glorified and compensated in this situation. His refusal solidified in Naaman's eyes that God was the healer—not Elisha.

Lust is a sin. Because we are New Testament prophets, it now includes intent and motives of the heart. Jesus said, *"Whoever looks at a woman to lust for her has already committed adultery with her in his heart"* (Matthew 5:28). Therefore, lust and spiritual adultery cannot be eliminated.

When hearing the word "lust," many people automatically think of "illicit sexual activity," but lust in its truest definition is "desiring anything that is outside the will of God for a person's life." He can call you to be a teacher, but you can lust after someone else's career as an actor or an actress. Lust has a broad scope and simply limiting it to sexual desires is drastically narrowing the scope of the word's expansive meaning.

We all have the propensity to want to satisfy our fleshly desires and whims. The Bible says sin is pleasurable for a season (Hebrews 11:25), and a human desires to live a life that is satisfying. From the pulpit to the pew, the church is swarming with what the philosopher, Dallas Willard, calls "Vampire Christians." All they want is to benefit from the blood of Jesus—not His Lordship.

We must strive to be prophets who desire obedience first; we cannot be resistant to God's instructions. The prophetic life is a process of consistent death. If you have yielded your life to Christ, you will constantly be under scrutiny. God desires a pure vessel and absolute holiness. We are not prophets who bow at the altar of selfish ambition.

18

WIRED TO BRING ORDER

As a marketplace prophet, it took me many years to find my niche. Most of the jobs I had were short-lived, and I was extremely bored until I landed my first job in a reputable health-care organization doing project management. Project management was an unheard-of profession in the 80's and 90's but one that is very popular today. Project management and quality control were so intriguing to me because the job offered me the opportunity to bring order to chaos, allowing me to take abstract data and make it into something meaningful.

According to Deuteronomy 34:10, Moses was the greatest prophet until Jesus, but he spent much of his time leading, teaching, settling disputes and organizing the people so that God's plan could be executed. This powerful principle tells me one of a prophet's greatest strengths is his ability to establish boundaries, order, and points of delineation.

Many times, in the Bible, God sanctioned a prophet to speak because things were out of order and not in sync with His plan. The Ten Commandments are a systematic document that brought order to worship because the people's worship was disorderly. So, for the past thirty years, I have found myself bringing order.

A word of admonition: prophet, don't be alarmed if everywhere you go is chaotic; it's God's plan, and you are on a divine assignment. My oldest daughter is a master communicator and educator who has struggled professionally because she says, "Everywhere I go, the people and companies are so unorganized." Exactly! So, God has used her tremendously in creating training structures and creating policy and procedures.

Prophets do not come onto the scene until it is time to build up or tear down a work. Every single church or organization to which God sent me was either newly established, changing their infrastructure or in the middle of a building program. I used to be irritated because I wanted to go somewhere that was nice and neat with everything in place, which of course, is far more comfortable than being caught in the middle of a spiritual collision.

In a healthy church or organization, a mature prophet can very quickly become an integral part of the core leadership. Prophets come alongside leadership and help keep the people engaged during times of upheaval and change. Due to their sensitivity to the Spirit and keen discernment, they can ward off sneak attacks from the enemy that would encumber growth and potentially cause discord among the people. They also add vibrancy, strength, and vigor to the people by refreshing them with their spiritual discipline and power-packed words.

As a marketplace prophet on a current assignment, I found myself struggling with my new boss, and I could not figure out why. I had a dream in which she told me to be back from lunch in 30 minutes. As I was trying to get back on time, I lost my keys, my purse and ended up in a completely unfamiliar building. I had to step away to see what the real problem was. If the prophet's gift is to bring order, then the enemy's counterattack is confusion.

Whenever God wanted to stop progress, He sent confusion. Deuteronomy 28:20 says, *"The LORD will send on you cursing, confusion, and rebuke in all that you set your hand to do."* The enemy has always mirrored and copied God's battle strategy. In a state of confusion, you cannot think clearly; you are disoriented, and you have trouble focusing on making decisions. Confusion is the enemy's attack, but the prophet's counterattack is establishing divine order.

19

INFALLIBLE

2 Timothy 3:16 says, *"All Scripture is given by inspiration of God, and is profitable for doctrine, for reproof, for correction, for instruction in righteousness."* The mode of transportation for the prophetic ministry is decreeing and declaring. Prophets have a responsibility to speak what they hear in the ear—not what they regurgitate from someone else. Jeremiah 23:30 says, *"'Therefore behold, I am against the prophets,' says the LORD, 'who steal My words everyone from his neighbor.'"* Additionally, a prophet must understand the authority that has been given to him from his mouth and the scriptures. Hebrews 4:12 (KJV) says:

> *For the word of God is quick, and powerful, and sharper than any two-edged sword, piercing even to the dividing asunder of soul and spirit, and of the joints and marrow, and is a discerner of the thoughts and intents of the heart.*

The word "two-edged" comes from the Greek word *distomos*[14], which literally means "two-mouthed" or "having two edges." The significance of a two-edged sword is that it was the perfect offensive and defensive weapon for any soldier. Also, known as "a drinker of blood," a two-edged sword penetrated its victim both going in and coming out.

The beauty of being a well-studied prophet is that he understands that the word in his mouth is the ultimate weapon and is used to edify, exhort, and comfort (1 Corinthians 14:3). His mouth is not a weapon to be used to manipulate and destroy God's people.

Hebrews 4:12 also confirms that the Bible is a living, breathing document, it is not outdated or irrelevant. Never trust a prophet who is not well acquainted with the scriptures. A prophet's responsibility is to meditate, recite, declare, study and read the Word of God, primarily to know the resonance of God's voice. God speaks on a specific frequency, and without investing time in His Word, a prophet's signals can get crossed. Many voices are clamoring to be heard and making sure you are hearing the right one is vitally important.

God's prophet must have a healthy and consistent diet of the Word since God will not prophesy anything that violates His Word. A prophet will always be able to validate the accuracy of his word if it is in line with the written Word. 2 Peter 1:20, 21 (LEB) says,

> *Recognizing this above all, that every prophecy of scripture does not come about from one's own interpretation, for no prophecy was ever produced by the will of man, but men carried along by the Holy Spirit spoke from God.*

Prophecy has never been birthed out of human ability but has always been the enablement of divine inspiration. The scripture warns the prophet about speaking words that are not divinely inspired. Deuteronomy 18:22 says,

> *When a prophet speaks in the name of the Lord, if the thing does not happen or come to pass, that is the thing which the Lord has not spoken; the prophet has spoken it presumptuously; you shall not be afraid of him.*

The passage in Hebrews also says the Word is *"A discerner of the thoughts and motives of the heart."* Most people never realize and apprehend this spiritual truth while reading the Word. As you study the Word, it is revealing to you the thoughts and motives of your heart that do not line up with what His Word says. A friend shared with me that God told her, "While you are reading the Word, the Word is reading you." The prophet must make sure that he operates from a pure and holy place. A prophet cannot live one life in private and another in public. An anonymous quote says, "I would rather be a public failure and a private success than be a public success and a private failure." Many do not read the Word because it brings conviction, which is one of the Holy Spirit's jobs. Never be a prophet who shuns correction. If you allow the Word to correct you, people generally will not have to.

To conclude, since there is an element in the prophet's ministry that is to the lost, it is important to be clear on what you believe and why. From an intellectual, theological, and academic position, you must be able to defend the scriptures clearly; many religions claim to be the truth. *So, What's the Difference* by Fritz Ridenour or *Kingdom of the Cults* by Walter Ralston Martin are excellent books to read on this subject.

20

BUILT TO LAST

In recent times, more people seem to be falling away from ministry than ever before. Reportedly over 1600 pastors and ministry leaders leave or are forced out of ministry each month, and over 7000 churches close each year. Pastors are discouraged, disillusioned, burned-out, experiencing financial problems, crumbling under the pressure of family responsibilities, and moral failures. Is this the divine plan of God? Or are there biblical principles, which can insulate prophets from the failure of ministry?

Ministry is a calling and a lifelong pursuit—not a vocation, and there is no earthly retirement plan. Your ministry is only as strong as you are. Paul, the apostle, told his protégé, Timothy,

> *So, my son, throw yourself into this work for Christ. Pass on what you heard from me…to reliable leaders who are competent to teach others. When the going gets rough, take it on the chin with the rest of us, the way Jesus did. A soldier on duty doesn't get caught up in making deals at the marketplace. He concentrates on carrying out orders. An athlete who refuses to play by the rules will never get anywhere. It's the diligent farmer who gets the produce. Think it over. God will make it all plain* (2 Timothy 2:2-7, MSG).

The following biblical principles will help establish a ministry that is built to last!

Attack or Distraction

Initially, you need to ascertain if the present situation is an attack against your destiny or a distraction. An attack is designed to destroy you. Distraction is a diversion or interruption. An attack has the potential to thwart your destiny and forward progress; a distraction is impotent and is merely a disturbance. In Nehemiah 6:3, Nehemiah responded to Sanballat, Tobiah, and Geshem the Arab's distraction by stating, *"I am doing a great work so that I cannot come down."* He responded to their attack by praying, "Give me strength."

In like fashion, a prophet is to respond to distraction by standing his ground and not changing his position. A prophet responds to an attack by soliciting God's help, staying connected to the house of God and by connecting with a Spirit-filled believer. Not even a prophet can overcome an attack alone.

Understanding Your Authority

You must irrefutably recognize you have power that is not of this world! You are powerless in your strength but invincible in God's strength. Luke 10:19 (AMP) says,

> *Listen carefully: I have given you authority [that you now possess] to tread on serpents and scorpions, and [the ability to exercise authority] over all the power of the enemy (Satan); and nothing will [in any way] harm you.*

Realizing this principle will save you some unnecessary wounds because you will no longer fight battles in your strength.

Maintain Your Prophetic Posture

The ministry of the prophet is an undercurrent. An *undercurrent*[15] is defined as "an underlying feeling or influence, especially one that is contrary to the prevailing atmosphere." A prophet will generally be going against the grain because prophets always live above the fray of public opinion. The prophets of old opposed the socio-economic and religious climate. In His day, Jesus, the Prophet, resisted the religious rhetoric of the Sadducees and Pharisees. What we declare cannot be driven by our emotions or personality.

PRACTICAL PROPHETIC LIVING

Endure Persecution

Persecution is inevitable and expected in the life of a believer and should not be a surprise or catch a believer off guard. He has promised in His Word: *"No weapon formed against you shall prosper, and every tongue which rises against you in judgment you shall condemn. This is the heritage of the servants of the LORD"* (Isaiah 54:17). Persecution and affliction are mechanisms God uses to produce growth, stability, and endurance. Exodus 1:12 says, *"But the more they afflicted them, the more they multiplied and grew."*

21

ADVANCING IN THE SPIRIT

One morning on my way to work, I was driving on a very congested freeway in Southern California. I had only advanced a few miles forward when I saw the same car I had seen two days earlier. I was not mistaken because the back window was broken. As I was driving, the Spirit of the Lord spoke to me and said, "Just because things look familiar doesn't mean you are in the same place." The Spirit of the Lord is confirming that you have gained ground and picked up momentum. You can enter your next season of productivity if you meet all the requirements.

First, believe in the promises of God. Romans 4:20 (KJV) says that Abraham *"Staggered not at the promise of God through unbelief; but was…fully persuaded that, what he had promised, he was able also to perform."* Accept that God requires that we believe not only in Him but what He says in His Word. Faith is not simply standing on the promises but using them as vehicles to your next destination.

Second, resist the temptation to be judgmental. Galatians 6:1 says, *"You who are spiritual restore such a one…lest you also be tempted."* Everyone who loves God has issues. We are all trying to work on what is not pleasing to Him. Because one of the functions of a prophet is standing in the gap for others, let prayer be your first response.

Third, do not look back. Luke 9:62 (NIV) says, *"Jesus replied, 'No one who puts a hand to the plow and looks back is fit for service in the kingdom of God.'"* Paul the apostle said, "I press on." Your mistakes can no longer determine the altitude at which you fly. The sin debt has already been paid, and God has extended mercy if you have truly repented. The story of Lot and his wife is a prime example of the consequences of looking back. His wife turned into a pillar of salt and perished because she did not heed God's instructions.

22

THE ART OF THE APOTHECARY

Ron Carpenter said, "So many people are trying to throw anointing oil up when the scriptures command it to flow down (Psalm 133:2)." The anointing of the Holy Spirit is the single-most important aspect of Christian ministry. Without the anointing on the life of a prophet, his ministry is dangerous, laborious, powerless, and ineffective. It is a requisite for all of those who serve, but the focus, in this book, is on those who carry a prophetic mantle.

So, what is the *anointing*? In the Old Testament, the anointing was represented by the oil, which was precisely blended by the perfumer or the apothecary. An apothecary was "a skilled shopkeeper who stored specific compounds and medicinal supplies to mix compounds, oils, and ointments." The mid-sixteenth century apothecaries are the equivalent of the modern-day pharmacists and chemists.

The anointing oil is a byproduct of holiness and not a blend that can be conjured up or mimicked. Also, the oil was used to anoint the tabernacle and its sacred vessels as well as to consecrate the priests into office. Without it, the sanctuary and the priests would have been unacceptable to God.

Exodus 30:22-33 (MSG) gives God's divine instruction to Moses:

> GOD spoke to Moses: "Take the best spices: twelve and a half pounds of liquid myrrh; half that much, six and a quarter pounds, of fragrant cinnamon; six and a quarter pounds of fragrant cane; twelve and a half pounds of cassia—using the standard Sanctuary weight for all of them—and a gallon of olive oil. Make these into a holy anointing oil, a perfumer's skillful blend.
>
> "Use it to anoint the Tent of Meeting, the Chest of The Testimony, the Table and all its utensils, the Lampstand and its utensils, the Altar of Incense, the Altar of Whole-Burnt-Offerings and all its utensils, and the

Washbasin and its base. Consecrate them so they'll be soaked in holiness so that anyone who so much as touches them will become holy.

"Then anoint Aaron and his sons. Consecrate them as priests to me. Tell the Israelites, 'This will be my holy anointing oil throughout your generations.' Don't pour it on ordinary men. Don't copy this mixture to use for yourselves. It's holy; keep it holy. Whoever mixes up anything like it, or puts it on an ordinary person, will be expelled."

Why would God speak to Moses about the specific ingredients to be used to create the Holy Anointing Oil and then use a seemingly unknown individual from the tribe of Judah, who was a skilled metalsmith to create it? Exodus 37:1, indicates that Bazaleel, whose name meant "in the shadow of God," continued the construction of the temple. Exodus 37:29 (KJV) reads *"And he made the holy anointing oil, and the pure incense of sweet spices, according to the work of the apothecary."* Thus, from the scripture references, we can see that God called select individuals to prepare the Holy Anointing Oil. He then gave divine revelation on how to prepare it.

Bezaleel did not have any previous training in making the Holy Anointing Oil. However, the scripture says it was compounded after the true art of the apothecary. This means that although Bezaleel did not have previous training in this trade, the required knowledge was imparted to him directly by the Spirit of God. The quality of the workmanship was the same as if he had been a master of the trade and *confirmed* by apothecary standards. This is how God works. The flesh cannot be involved. Ecclesiastes 10:1 (KJV) says, *"Dead flies cause the ointment of the apothecary to send forth a stinking savour."*

Hence, how do these instructions translate to New Testament prophets? The anointing oil was a smearing and a rubbing on of oil to empower an individual for service or to accomplish a task.
Our New Testament prophet Jesus declared the following in Luke 4:18, *"The Spirit of the LORD is upon Me, because He has anointed Me to preach the gospel to the poor; He has sent Me to heal the brokenhearted, to proclaim liberty to the captives and recovery of sight to the blind, to set at liberty those who are oppressed."*

PRACTICAL PROPHETIC LIVING

1 John 2:20 says, *"But you have an anointing from the Holy One, and you know all things."* This verse confirms that the Holy Spirit has empowered a believer for a specific purpose. Everything needed to fulfill the God-given assignment is already embedded in the person's spiritual genetics. God anoints an individual to do something significant.

The anointing that you have received will also train you, teach you and give you the necessary tools that you need to accomplish your divine destiny. As previously addressed, God selected the specific ingredients that would make up the holy anointing oil. In the Old Testament, the ingredients were literal; in the New Testament, they are spiritual.

PRACTICAL PROPHETIC LIVING

The chart below expounds on the characteristics of the individual ingredients in the holy anointing oil and how they apply to us today.

Spice	Amount	History	Characteristic of the anointing
Myrrh	500 shekels	o In the ancient world, it was worth more than its weight in gold. o It was used to heal and bring relief from pain. o It was used to anoint Jesus' body for burial. o It was burned by the Romans to cover the stench of burning flesh. o When the spice was heated, it expanded and bloomed.	o Costly. o Prepares you for death and then covers its stench. o Heals and relieves pain. o Purifies. o Perfumes.
Sweet Cinnamon and Cassia	750 shekels	o The oil is extracted by pounding and maceration (causing constituents to breakdown by using water). o The spice was very fragrant. o It added flavor to food. o It was given to Potentates as a gift.	o Must encounter water (the spirit) to be used. o Be of a good reputation, able to add flavor. o It will bring you into to the presence of influential people.

PRACTICAL PROPHETIC LIVING

Spice	Amount	History	Characteristic of the anointing
Calamus	250 shekels	o It was used for medicinal purposes. o The flowers have a putrid smell and only give off a sweet odor when the leaves are broken.	o It heals. o It must be broken to be fragrant.
Olive oil	Hin	o The tree can endure long seasons of drought. o It grows slowly, and the fruit ripens slowly. o The tree can last for centuries and still be fruitful (some trees have been reported to be over 1000 years old). o The oil is produced by adding weight. o It was used to anoint athletes and kings. o The most important ingredients in producing fruitful olive trees are sun, stone, drought, silence, and solitude: o The trees have sturdy and extensive root systems. o An essential element for blending	o It enables a person to endure periods where God seems far off. o It takes time to produce. o It provides longevity (generally what we see is a gift in operation; the anointing lasts and endures). o It enables a person to withstand great pressure and still produce something valuable and useful. o Produces sweet fellowship.

23

THE MARKS OF A MATURE PROPHET

Maturity in a prophet is paramount. Novice prophets rarely understand their function, or the necessary preparations required to be effective in Christian ministry. People are a prophet's canvas, and they must be handled with care. I have seen many people badly hurt by immature prophets who had no filters or restraints. As my prophetic gift began to become operative, I thought I was supposed to speak everything that came to my mind and tell everyone what I saw or sensed in the spirit. I did not have the maturity to understand that some of what I saw was for the sake of prayer and not for me to verbalize every time I felt I had a message to convey.

    If I could turn back the clock, I would have sought God more and asked Him: "Is this for me to share or pray about?" If the Word is for me to share, then the Holy Spirit will speak to the person before I share it with them. If the matter is for me to pray about, then the matter will remain private for the Holy Spirit to do the work. I have highlighted some characteristics that are woven into the mantle of a mature prophet.

A Love for Mankind

    Jonah was disobedient. The moment he heard God's voice, Jonah 1:3 says Jonah fled from the presence of the Lord. He believed that he could resist the instruction of God because he did not like the people to whom God was sending him. He felt that because of the nature of the Ninevites, they did not deserve God's mercy. The fact that the people believed in God angered the prophet. Obedience is so crucial in the life of a prophet because he may be commanded to speak to people that he doesn't believe deserve the mercy of God.

    David Berkowitz, nicknamed the Son of Sam, was a satanic serial killer whose reign of terror ended on August 15, 1977, after killing six people and wounding seven. I remember listening to *Focus on the Family* with Dr. James Dobson, who was conducting a three-day interview with Berkowitz that was riveting. (That three-day interview is available on YouTube called the "Son of Hope.") What would have happened to David Berkowitz's soul if Dr. Dobson had declined meeting with him? John 3:16 is not contingent on a person's behavior but on Christ's undying love and gruesome sacrifice. *For God so loved the world,* including David Berkowitz.

In a later interview with CBN, Berkowitz said the memories still haunted him, but he had given his life to Jesus Christ. When asked by an interviewer, "Did you want to get caught?" he answered, "I wanted to get delivered. I wanted to get delivered. I was living without hope. I had surrendered myself to…serve the Devil." Although he ritualistically murdered and wounded people, God still had a plan for his life; he became the son of hope. The redemption of mankind is our greatest focus, and obedience to divine instruction is a deadly weapon against the enemy.

Humility

A prophet's only concern should be that God's message is heard. It is so easy for a prophet to want everyone to know his name and be given credit, especially in the age of social media. However, the ministry does not belong to the prophet; the ministry belongs to God. A prophet is merely a vessel. Because the prophetic ministry has tremendous drawing power, it can be very easy to get caught up and allow pride to creep in.

A prophet operating in pride is a deadly poison that can destroy a church brick by brick. He will undermine the pastor and church leaders in an effort to be known and be significant. James 4:10 should be a mainstay in the prayer arsenal of a prophet. The verse commands us to allow God to do the lifting and not our gifting: *"Humble yourselves before the Lord, and he will lift you up in honor"* (NLT).

1 Chronicles 16:22 is probably the most misused scripture when it comes to prophetic ministry. Everywhere prophets are declaring, *"Do My prophets no harm."* An uncircumcised prophet tends to believe that because of this scripture, he has some special privilege and is above correction.

PRACTICAL PROPHETIC LIVING

Economist and author Ron McKenzie said,

> We must be careful about building a theology of prophetic privilege. God has not promised to protect His prophets, but He will protect His Word. Jesus warned that prophets would be persecuted. He did not say they *should* be protected. It is very important to keep a right perspective of ourselves and the ministry God has entrusted to us.

Popularity is not the mark of a true prophet, and people will rarely speak well of a prophet. Popularity and fame are the marks of a false prophet. *"Woe to you when all men speak well of you, for so did their fathers to the false prophets"* (Luke 6:26).

A Tamed Tongue

A prophet's mouth is the vehicle God uses to shift atmospheres and bring deliverance and healing to His people. God determines the message, not the prophet. A prophet is His spokesperson, and the condition of his tongue is of the utmost importance. Just like God used Moses in Exodus 3:14 to declare a message to His people, He is still using prophets today.

A prophet's words can have a crippling effect on people and guarding what he says helps protect the validity and credibility of the ministry the prophet stewards. Psalm 141:3 contains one of my constant declarations to God: *"Set a guard, O LORD, over my mouth; Keep watch over the door of my lips."*

Because God still speaks through His prophets today, they do not have the luxury of speaking their minds. He must sanctify his lips and guard every word that comes out of his mouth. The words coming out of a prophet's mouth cannot be a mixture of the holy and the profane. James 3:8-12 admonishes every believer:

> *But no man can tame the tongue. It is an unruly evil, full of deadly poison. With it, we bless our God and Father, and with it, we curse men, who have been made in the similitude of God. Out of the same mouth proceed blessing*

and cursing. My brethren, these things ought not to be so. Does a spring send forth fresh water and bitter from the same opening? Can a fig tree, my brethren, bear olives, or a grapevine bear figs? Thus, no spring yields both salt water and fresh.

They Understand Who They Are

According to a previous chapter, it is essential for prophets to understand they are sons. A prophet is created in the image of God, and He is the model that prophets follow. When a prophet lacks identity, he will mimic and copy other ministries instead of developing his own unique expression. Prophets tend to struggle with envy, jealousy, and comparison. The one thing that will kill a prophet's ministry is falling prey to these deadly snares. Regarding comparison, Paul admonished the church at Corinth that comparing yourself to your peers is unwise (2 Corinthians 10:12.). Andy Stanley, the pastor of North Point Church, said,

> There's no win in comparison. Let's face it. Not a day goes by that you're not tempted to glance to the left and to the right to see how you measure up to the people around you. But it doesn't stop there, does it? You're tempted to compare your children to other children, your spouse to other spouses! It's frustrating. It's exhausting. It's a TRAP!

I talk with many prophets who do not think they are prophets because they do not sound like, preach like or exhort like another. The danger of this comparison is that the prophet doing the comparing may never complete his assignment if he believes the validity of his ministry is tied to how he exercises his gift. God does not create copies; rather, He creates individuals, and the expression of everyone's gift will be in line with his unique personality. Psalm 139:14 declares, *"I will praise You, for I am fearfully and wonderfully made; Marvelous are Your works, and that my soul knows very well."* This Psalm reinforces the fact that each person is distinct in every aspect of his being.

PRACTICAL PROPHETIC LIVING

I used to struggle with preaching forcefully, and as a result, I would try to be quiet and demure because I thought that was the proper way to be. I remember ministering at a church when, instead of flowing with my communication style, I decided I would try to mimic someone else. When I finished my message, my kids looked at me and said, "Who was that? That did not even sound like you." Because my children were so accustomed to my ministering, they could tell the difference between phony and authentic. I vowed never to do that again and had to learn to accept the fact my preaching and teaching style was God-ordained.

Anchored in Love

Prophets, more than any other gifting, need to be rooted and anchored in love. The prophetic personality only sees two colors: black or white. There is no middle ground; things are either right or wrong. Because of this disposition, the prophet has a strong tendency to become very judgmental and critical. A prophet is very comfortable with confronting sin publicly and has very little patience for people who continue in it.

As partakers in the new covenant of grace, prophets must make sure that as they correct and exhort, they always leave the door open for a person to reconcile with Christ. Regardless of the office the prophet holds, according to the apostle Paul:

> *All this is from God, who reconciled us to himself through Christ and gave us the ministry of reconciliation: that God was reconciling the world to himself in Christ, not counting people's sins against them. And he has committed to us the message of reconciliation* (2 Corinthians 5:18, 19, NIV).

Lovers of the Church

Loving the church of Jesus Christ is a prerequisite for being a healthy, functional, and effective prophet. The reality of today is that many ministries do not understand the prophetic gift, and prophets tend to be the first ones who get hurt or overlooked. The prophet must remember that if God sent him to a church, He sent him for a reason. People there need the ministry that He has entrusted to His prophet. Therefore, the prophet must remain steadfast and vigilant in the work because people's lives are at stake.

When a healthy church overlooks the prophetic gift, mainly because of ignorance, the prophets begin to flock to churches that are full of rejected prophets. This is very dangerous because the standard of the Gospel is rarely enforced and because the pastor does not want to offend, it creates a culture of rebellion. It becomes a spiritual club and a social gathering. Prophets are so acquainted with rejection that when they find a place where they can breathe and belong, they put down roots. As a prophet, you are obligated to keep the standard raised; it does not lower because you are still struggling with certain issues. If these issues are pressing and the bondage is beyond your ability to overcome, the proper recourse is sitting yourself down until you are healed.

Rootless prophets do not carry the heart of the Father. Their mission is far more important than God's. Those observing can see these prophets rapidly digress in their spiritual vitality. Two important reasons for staying connected are found in the book of Proverbs: *"As iron sharpens iron, so a man sharpens the countenance of his friend"* (Proverbs 27:17) and *"A man who isolates himself seeks his own desire; he rages against all wise judgment"* (Proverbs 18:1).

The prophet who isolates himself loses the privilege of being corrected and vetted by other believers. Vetting is an important part of the Christian life as every prophet needs other believers to authenticate the validity of his prophetic ministry. The prophet's level of education, how gifted he is or his tenure in the church has no bearing on his validity because becoming disenchanted with the ministry and skewing the scriptures can be easily done. Another reason for staying connected is not to neglect or overlook the fragrance of sweet fellowship with the saints. Fellowshipping with God's people is a privilege, and it allows prophets to remain spiritually healthy. Hebrews 10:24-25 (AMP) urges,

> *and let us consider [thoughtfully] how we may encourage one another to love and to do good deeds, not forsaking our meeting together [as believers*

for worship and instruction], as is the habit of some, but encouraging one another; and all the more [faithfully] as you see the day [of Christ's return] approaching.

When a prophet becomes disillusioned, he can easily become heretical, self-righteous, and difficult to correct. No doubt you have heard people quote the statement attributed to Valerie Irick Rainford: "It doesn't matter where you start but how you finish that matters!" You can start off well and end badly. Through the years, many have started well in ministry and then rapidly declined because of an offense or an indiscretion. Ministry is all prophets know, and it can be very lucrative. As a result, they do everything they can to keep the machine running. A prophet can easily relinquish his position as one of God's prophets. His gift can remain intact, but he no longer represents God; he represents one person—himself. As a mentor who heals prophetic people, staying connected to a healthy church is my first instruction. A prophet who isolates himself is heading for destruction.

Understands Their Jurisdiction

In 2 Corinthians 10:13 (NIV), we see that Paul understood to whom he was called and when. He wrote under the inspiration of the Holy Spirit, *"We, however, will not boast beyond proper limits, but will confine our boasting to the sphere of service God himself has assigned to us, a sphere that also includes you."* I was taught that a prophet has authority where he has responsibility. In other words, no responsibility, no authority. Since prophets are very intuitive people, they see more than the average churchgoer. But everything they see is not for them to fix.

Since prophets can struggle with pushy personalities and have the proclivity to be controlling, they can override the jurisdiction in which they have been assigned. There are times when the Holy Spirit will restrict you, and as a prophet, you must be sensitive and obedient enough to trust the Holy Spirit's leading. On one of Paul's missionary journeys, he was instructed by the Spirit not to go to Jerusalem. There is no explanation why, nor did Paul seek one, he just obeyed. Acts 21:1-4 says,

> *Now it came to pass, that when we had departed from them and set sail, running a straight course we came to Cos, the following day to Rhodes, and from there to Patara. And finding a ship sailing over to Phoenicia, we went aboard and set sail. When we had sighted Cyprus, we passed it on the left, sailed to Syria, and landed at Tyre; for there the ship was to unload her cargo. And finding disciples, we stayed there seven days. They told Paul through the Spirit not to go up to Jerusalem.*

Your sphere of influence grows as you mature, but you must be dedicated to the assignments you have been given and steward the people within those assignments well. Through this, God measures your maturity and faithfulness.

I initially started my ministry in music as a choir member, a praise and worship leader and later a choir administrator. Initially, the only authority I had was myself. I had to master *me* before I could govern anyone else. I had to make sure I knew my songs, I attended rehearsals, I was at every assigned service, and I was a faithful member of my church. As my ministry began to grow, I became the director of the altar worker's ministry at another church. At that point, I could not be concerned about what was going on in the children's ministry or any other ministry. My jurisdiction was the altar worker's ministry.

Now, I operate my own ministry and have traveled nationally and internationally. But I understand my jurisdiction and stay within the confines of my ministry. Although I started off in the music ministry, God was moving me systematically towards my purpose. Unknown to me, my destination and God's ultimate purpose was for me to heal, mature, and train prophets.

24

INHERENT QUALITIES

The prophetic personality is very distinctive. In Carl J. Jung's psychological theory[16] (Jung, 1971), the author teaches that people's personalities are based on their general attitude, their perception and how they judge life around them. According to Jung, sixteen different personality types exist. From Jung's list of personality types, the prophet seems to most embody the "INFJ" personality. The caveat is that the absence or presence of these characteristics does not necessarily determine whether a person is prophetic but is used as a point of reference. This personality description fits the biblical prophets. I have not encountered a prophet who does not have this basic psychological makeup.

According to Myers & Briggs, a mother and daughter team[17] who researched personality types, this personality type is characterized by I—Introversion, N—Intuition, F—Feeling, and J—Judgment. INFJs have complex personalities who rely on intuition and emotions to advocate for what they believe in. Their complexity can be seen in the life of the prophet Ezekiel, about whom R. Loren Sandford wrote the following:

> Prophetic personalities often have little consciousness of what might be seen by others to be weird behavior, and they may tend to communicate in ways that neither they nor others fully understand. John the Baptist wore camel skin and ate bugs! Hardly normal behavior! Ezekiel dug holes in the city wall and carried his travel baggage around all day just for people to see (Ezekiel 12). And that was nothing compared to Ezekiel 4 where he built a toy city in the public place, and then laid down by it for the better part of 430 days. If that were not enough, he had himself tied up with ropes. He did all this just to proclaim the siege and destruction of Jerusalem and the deportation of the population into exile. "Normal" people would never entertain such instructions as coming from God.

Interestingly, this personality type is extremely rare, and according to several sources, only represents 1 percent of the population. That statistic alone tells me that though many will call themselves prophets, there are very few in each generation. Matthew 24:11 (KJV) says, *"And many false prophets shall rise, and shall deceive many."*

According to Myers & Briggs, the INFJ personality is known as the "Protector."[18] The strengths of this personality include a strong intuitive nature, very resourceful, philanthropic, highly principled and very inspiring. These highly gifted individuals can sometimes make interaction with them very difficult, if not impossible because everything in their world is an absolute; there are no gray areas. They are very verbal when they believe they are right and dominate conversations. They are extremely pushy when it comes to expressing their ideas, but remember, it is because they believe their ideas are solely for the greater good. It is very important for a "protector" personality to apply the admonition of James 1:19 (KJV) consistently, *"Let every man be swift to hear, slow to speak, slow to wrath."*

Their weaknesses position this personality type to struggle with anxiety, stress, and depression. They also tend to battle with the validity of their ministry. Most of the people I have met who possess prophetic gifts tend to shy away from them. As discussed, they struggle with rebellion as characterized in the life of Moses who struck the rock instead of speaking to it as God had directed him (Numbers 20:11). This rebellion was also present in the life of Jonah who did not want his assignment and bargained with God for reassignment.

This personality type can also make it difficult for prophets to maintain intimate relationships. The personality is weakened by being very judgmental and critical. Therefore, prophets must consistently apply the mercy of God. A disciplined walk of love will help thwart this natural inclination. In Ephesians 4:32, Paul commands, *"Be kind to one another, tenderhearted, forgiving one another, even as God in Christ forgave you."*

In ministry, prophets tend to be more concerned about the ministry of the Holy Spirit in operation than the cry of the people. Prophets understand if they yield to the Holy Spirit, God will answer the cry of the people. They push people toward intimacy with God. Their ministry focus is prayer, fasting, and healing. They are natural worshippers and hunger for the presence of God. They are restrained by holiness and righteousness and abhor disobedience in themselves and others. The pure prophetic gift manifests itself in preaching, writing, and exhortation. Prophets are God's response to social injustice, rebellion, and heresy. Prophets are on God's schedule, and He chooses their assignment.

They are acutely aware of the presence of sin and unrighteousness and are very sensitive to a lack of authenticity and dishonesty. Prophets are bearers of the truth and are more loyal to the truth than they are to people. Cutting off relationships and moving on is very easy for them because their commitment to the truth can cause them to be spiritual nomads. With the help of the Holy Spirit, the challenges related to this personality type can be greatly diminished as the prophet becomes more comfortable in his skin and identifies the triggers that cause these negative traits to flourish.

25

ARMED AND READY

Rick Jenner, the author of *Dressed to Kill, A Biblical Approach to Spiritual Warfare and Armor* wrote,

> Any person who has been in touch with the national pulse of the church would quickly agree that at times, the Body of Christ experiences what I have come to call a "spiritual warfare mania."
>
> This emphasis on spiritual warfare is *good* in that it causes us to become familiar with our adversary, the devil, and how he operates. Once we understand his mode of operation, we can then foil his attacks against us. This is the very reason Paul told the Corinthians concerning the devil and his mode of operation, *"...We are not ignorant of his [Satan's] devices"* (2 Corinthian 2:11).

Spiritual warfare is "the act of taking a stand against the forces of evil." The operative word is *stand;* we were never instructed in the scriptures to fight. God told Jehoshaphat in 2 Chronicles 20:17, *"You will not need to fight in this battle. Position yourselves, stand still and see the salvation of the Lord."* The Psalmist David appealed to Jehovah Sabaoth, the Lord of Host and the Captain of the army in Psalms 35:1-2 which reads, *"Plead my cause, O Lord, with those who strive with me; Fight against those who fight against me. Take hold of shield and buckler, and stand up for my help."*

The conflict between good and evil has been the battle of the ages, and God uses His prophets to overcome the forces of evil in very demonstrative ways. The important point to remember is that a prophet is never alone. It does not matter how intense the battle becomes, God is with His servant. When the king of Syria was making war against Israel, the prophet Elijah was battle ready. When the Syrian army surrounded Israel, Elisha did not flinch. He commanded the young man not to fear. 2 Kings 6:16-18 records:

> *So, he answered, "Do not fear, for those who are with us are more than those who are with them." And Elisha prayed, and said, "LORD, I pray, open his eyes that he may see." Then the LORD opened the eyes of the young man, and he saw. And behold, the mountain was full of horses and chariots of fire all around Elisha. So, when the Syrians came down to him, Elisha prayed to the LORD, and said, "Strike this people, I pray, with blindness." And He struck them with blindness according to the word of Elisha.*

Amid great pressure, Elijah stood alone as the sole prophet of God against the 450 prophets of Baal. 1 Kings 18:36-40 documents the power of Elijah's prayer:

> *And it came to pass, at the time of the offering of the evening sacrifice, that Elijah the prophet came near and said, "LORD God of Abraham, Isaac, and Israel, let it be known this day that You are God in Israel and I am Your servant and that I have done all these things at Your word. Hear me, O LORD, hear me, that this people may know that You are the LORD God, and that You have turned their hearts back to You again." Then the fire of the LORD fell and consumed the burnt sacrifice, and the wood and the stones and the dust, and it licked up the water that was in the trench. Now when all the people saw it, they fell on their faces; and they said, "The LORD, He is God! The LORD, He is God!" And Elijah said to them, "Seize the prophets of Baal! Do not let one of them escape!" So, they seized them; and Elijah brought them down to the Brook Kishon and executed them there.*

Prophets are innately skilled in battle, and an equipped prophet is armed, dangerous and ready to strike at a moment's notice.

26

MANAGING THE PROPHETIC FAMILY

Family genes are powerful. Just like natural traits are passed down from our parents, so are spiritual traits. Just like I inherited my mother's eyes and my father's hair, I acquired my family's prophetic gifts. My mother had a very strong prophetic gift, and so do all my siblings. My children have very strong prophetic gifts as well. That does not necessarily mean they will walk in the office of a prophet as I do because God has a plan and purpose specific to them.

Moses' family is the biblical prototype of a prophetic family. Numbers 26:59 says, *"The name of Amram's wife was Jochebed the daughter of Levi, who was born to Levi in Egypt; and to Amram she bore Aaron and Moses and their sister Miriam."* God earmarked Moses as one of the greatest prophets to ever live (Deuteronomy 34:10); his sister Miriam was a prophetess (Numbers 26:59), and his brother Aaron was also a prophet (Exodus 7:1).

Based on the prophetic personality information provided in a previous chapter, the prophetic household can be extremely volatile and conflict-driven. Their intuitive and sensitive nature can make the home a bastion for offense and rejection. Numbers 12:1-5 details the conflict between Moses, Miriam, and Aaron because they were not happy with Moses' choice for a wife:

> *Then Miriam and Aaron spoke against Moses because of the Ethiopian woman whom he had married; for he had married an Ethiopian woman. So, they said, "Has the LORD indeed spoken only through Moses? Has He not spoken through us also?" And the LORD heard it. (Now the man Moses was very humble, more than all men who were on the face of the earth.) Suddenly the LORD said to Moses, Aaron, and Miriam, "Come out, you three, to the tabernacle of meeting!" So, the three came out. Then the LORD came down in the pillar of cloud and stood in the door of the tabernacle, and called Aaron and Miriam. And they both went forward.*

Also, the complexity of the prophetic personality and propensity toward depression can hinder healthy communication within the family setting, which can open the door to deep feelings of rejection on top of what a prophet already experiences by nature of the call. I tried to be diligent about creating an environment of acceptance in our home.

I found there are two essentials in managing a prophetic home. First, it is important to keep the lines of communication clear. It is so easy to allow ourselves to be consumed with life that we are all like ships passing in the night and forget how important connecting with one another is. Second, it is important to create an environment of love and acceptance which will help ward off the effects of sibling rivalry. If you only have one child help them accept who they are and insulate them from the dangers of comparison as discussed in a previous chapter.

On the other hand, because prophets are very service-oriented and crave intimacy, the family of the prophet tends to be very close-knit. My children and I have often heard, "We look like brother and sister." I have never thought about the fact that it appears that way because of the intimacy and closeness of our relationship. They respect me as their mother but also feel the comfort and assurance of sharing some of their life experiences as well as seeking advice from me.

27

MINISTERING TO THE PROPHETIC HUSBAND

Although prophets are more comfortable in monogamous relationships, many times, in marriage they prefer peace, solitude and can easily be agitated by the presence of people. While enjoying his personal space, he will often be satisfied and acutely aware of his spouse's existence. Despite their desire for solitude, they can cling to their spouse for emotional support during difficult seasons.

Not pressuring this personality type to communicate is important as they do not like conflict and avoid difficult conversations. Despite avoiding conflict, they can have explosive bouts of anger when pressured. Therefore, it is important to learn how to resolve differences amicably, so resentment and bitterness are not allowed to take root. Since a great deal of spiritual warfare around the prophetic man can occur, it is important for the prophet's wife to be skilled in prayer. Interceding for a prophetic spouse can be hindered if bitterness can take root. For that reason, forgiveness is fundamental in the prophetic marriage.

In addition, the prophetic spouse can be very complex emotionally and mentally but simple when it comes to life. Since they are introverts, they love attention and crave deep emotional connections with others. Although they can appear to be moody and isolated, they are very sensitive and must be handled with care. They may not be verbally expressive of their love, but because prophets tend to be service-oriented, they will reward their mates emotionally with simple acts of kindness and affection.

Moreover, I believe, prophets should marry prophets because a lot of effort is required for a prophet to remain in intimate relationships with people other than prophets. Marrying a prophet, in my opinion, is the ideal situation, but prophets also work well with people who are innovative, inventive and have a voracious thirst for knowledge.

Since we are God's mouthpiece, guarding our words as a prophetic wife and mother are vital in sustaining a healthy marriage and family. Our words cannot be used as tools to manipulate our spouses into doing what we want them to do. A wife must refrain from using her words as emotional weapons. Colossians 4:6 says, *"Let your speech always be with grace, seasoned with salt, that you may know how you ought to answer each one."* Because we are driven toward holiness and righteousness, we can push our families too hard. This prophetic pushiness can hinder the growth and maturity of our families causing profound feelings of imperfection.

Because I am in public ministry, I must constantly remind myself that at home, I am a wife and a mother. I cannot allow my public ministry to bleed into my responsibilities at home. Also, being diligent about my emotional health affords me the ability not to take everything personally which enables me to effectively steward my home.

28

SAFEGUARDING THE PROPHETIC CHILD

Moses' mother, Jochebed, understood all too well her responsibility in safeguarding her son's life and protecting his calling. Moses' mother had three prophetic children, so she must have had some insight into God's purpose for their lives. When Pharaoh decreed that all the Hebrew boys born had to be thrown into the Nile (Exodus 1:22), Jochebed and Moses' sister, Miriam, began devising a plan for Moses' protection. By this time, Aaron was already three years old (Exodus 7:7), which is why he was not a target of Pharaoh's extermination plan. Moses' birth converged with Pharaoh's plan to destroy all male Hebrew children. He was marked from birth. Exodus 2:1-8 records,

> *And a man of the house of Levi went and took as wife a daughter of Levi. So, the woman conceived and bore a son. And when she saw that he was a beautiful child, she hid him three months. But when she could no longer hide him, she took an ark of bulrushes for him, daubed it with asphalt and pitch, put the child in it, and laid it in the reeds by the river's bank. And his sister stood afar off, to know what would be done to him. Then the daughter of Pharaoh came down to bathe at the river. And her maidens walked along the riverside; and when she saw the ark among the reeds, she sent her maid to get it. And when she opened it, she saw the child, and behold, the baby wept. So, she had compassion on him, and said, "This is one of the Hebrews' children." Then his sister said to Pharaoh's daughter, "Shall I go and call a nurse for you from the Hebrew women, that she may nurse the child for you?" And Pharaoh's daughter said to her, "Go." So, the maiden went and called the child's mother.*

Therefore, a mother's or father's primary responsibility in rearing a prophetic child is safeguarding his spirit and cultivating his call. The demonic assault can open the door to profound emotional issues and possibly mental illness. Prophetic people must master the art of managing what they see in the spirit realm with what is happening in the natural realm. Children do not have the spiritual or emotional capacity or maturity to do that. Every prophet in the Bible had visions or spiritual encounters. Samuel, the boy prophet, heard voices (1 Samuel 3:4, 6, 8, 10). Without Eli, Samuel could have become very confused because 1 Samuel 3:6 says that Samuel did not yet know the Lord. Daniel had visions and interpreted dreams (Daniel 2:19-24). Isaiah saw a vision of the Lord when King Uzziah died (Isaiah 6:1).

As a child, my nightmares contained a reoccurring theme. I remember having the same dream over and over for weeks and maybe even months. My memory of someone chasing me into a large castle is as vivid today as it was forty years ago. Several times, I encountered dark forces, which left me frightened and fearful. I also experienced crushing rejection from the people around me.

Children will be children and siblings naturally have conflict, but a prophetic family should be very sensitive and watchful that the enemy is not trying to emotionally cripple their children through these encounters. I was very watchful and vehement about not creating sibling rivalry. Although this competition can occur naturally, a parent can exacerbate the situation by favoring one child over another.

As these family dynamics, coupled with my dysfunction played out, my youngest daughter and oldest son probably experienced the most spiritual and emotional conflict. This struggle left my youngest daughter feeling very ostracized and alone. I remember one evening when she was nearly ten years of age, and we were leaving a Bible study, the Holy Spirit told me to tell her, "You are not the black sheep of the family."

"I always thought I was," she responded.

God intervened in her life in a very demonstrative way. She is now 24, and I have had to continually speak those words for her to hear and reinforce her spirit.

My oldest son had an encounter with an angel when he was five years old, which made him avoid spiritual matters altogether. He shared that when he got up to go to the bathroom one night, he saw a smiling man wearing a white robe standing at the bathroom door.

PRACTICAL PROPHETIC LIVING

"Were you afraid?" I asked.

"No," he answered.

His answer told me that what he saw was not a demonic spirit since the very nature of Satan is fear. The man looked at him and said, "Everything is going to be all right." Which much later, during a heavy season of testing, would prove to be the anchor we held on to.

My son said the angel went into our daughters' room, looked at them and exited through their bedroom window, which only confirmed my belief that my children had an angelic visitation. Because the window was so close to the ground, their father had nailed it shut so no one could climb in while they were asleep. These two encounters kept me constantly interceding for God's presence in their lives and their salvation.

Secondarily, your responsibility as a parent is to ensure they understand what their prophetic responsibility is in this life. You must ensure their moral compass is calibrated correctly and position them to accept the fact that they are agents of change in whatever arena God sets them. Most importantly, it is your job to birth a hunger in them for the Word of God. The Word must be their first reaction to life's challenges.

Personally, my birth family was full of crippled prophets. We did not have this spiritual safeguard; my siblings and I experienced an abundance of spiritual torment and emotional and sexual abuse. Our family was plagued with some form of drug addiction and/or mental illness. I can contribute some of our issues to generational iniquities, but I contribute the bulk of our issues to unmanaged prophetic gifts and having parents who did not understand our family's spiritual responsibility.

29

EXCELLING IN THE WORKPLACE

Statistics say only 1 to 2 percent of the people work in the church; the other 98 percent, or so, are in the marketplace. I spent thirty years as a marketplace prophet, and I watched God prosper me and create opportunities to minister His love and salvation to people. I once heard a man give his testimony about wanting to be in full-time ministry. He said, "I would pray to God every day to open the door for ministry. One day, God spoke to me and said, 'Your job is your ministry.'"

That man's testimony ministered to me because it took me many years to embrace the fact that God needed me right where I was. For years, I felt like I was leading a double life—ministry on the weekends and diligently working my job on the weekdays. Ministering to God's people was my passion, and I felt my job was an unwelcome distraction that was interfering with my *real* life.

As a prophet, your function is not only in the church. Some prophets are strictly assigned to the marketplace, and they must learn how to manage people and not hurt them. As a marketplace prophet, God used me to speak into people's lives, but it had to be strategic because I still had to honor the ethics of the company for which I worked and perform the work I had been hired to do. A Christian employer once said, "I don't like to hire Christians because they don't work. They spend their time doing ministry." In addition, I had to ensure that the person receiving the ministry was in a good place to receive it and did not cause undue emotional interruption.

Not until I embraced the concept of my job being my ministry did I begin to evangelize the marketplace. I had the opportunity to take breaks and lunch with people who needed a touch from Him. I prayed for, ministered to, gave direction, and loved God's people in the marketplace. As a result, lives were changed.

In one instance, my former boss' husband was diagnosed with liver and pancreatic cancer. He later went on to be with the Lord, but I was grateful that my husband and I had the opportunity to be with them during that time in their lives. Shortly after he passed, both my boss and I moved on to other positions. I wanted to move on from that position several times, but God kept me there until my assignment was complete.

I witnessed the hand of God use me to save marriages, save families and train budding prophets. I would encourage those reading this book to let God use you where you are. He knows when you are ready to transition into something more fulfilling if you are not already in an effectual place of service.

Commonly, the prophetic person tends to be entrepreneurial and desires either to be in full-time ministry or have his own business. However, I must stress: let God be your guide. As I am writing this book, I only recently transitioned into a space where I can prepare myself for full-time ministry as well as launch my own company. Before transitioning out of the marketplace, I often lamented about being done. I was so ready to throw in the towel and move on, but a prophet came to me and said, "You may be done, but you are not released." I had to wait for God's divine release patiently, and that liberation took one more year.

If you are a prophet called to the marketplace, understanding that education can open the door but only the anointing on your life will move you forward is important. This generation has been duped into thinking that education is equivalent to anointing. Education is important and provides a platform from which to start, but the anointing and favor of God cause a person to excel in his workplace ministry.

I was not as formally educated as my peers, but I learned more from experience. Although at times, I felt inferior because of my lack of formal education, the Spirit of God taught me that a person with an anointing is far more superior to a person with a degree. The prophet Isaiah said, *"The Sovereign LORD has given me a well-instructed tongue, to know the word that sustains the weary. He wakens me morning by morning, wakens my ear to listen like one being instructed (Isaiah 50:4)."*

While in the marketplace, I watched God move me from earning minimum wage to well over six figures. I watched God teach me how to communicate with those far more educated than me. Like a well-strategized chess game, He placed me in front of the right people at the right time. He gave me the perfect assignments that allowed me to shine. He was faithful, and I tried to be as faithful to Him by being a good employee.

As a child, I had aspirations of becoming a scientist. I also loved history and absorbed information from our set of encyclopedias. Then I became a sports enthusiast and wanted to do sports medicine; however, by the time I finished high school, I enrolled in college to study the field of engineering. On a whim, I ended up getting my certification in bookkeeping. You see, God had another plan and knew the exact profession that would fit my prophetic personality and call.

So, what jobs are good for marketplace prophets? I ended up working in the healthcare industry for thirty years. According to studies, the primary jobs that are gratifying for prophets or INJF's are ministry-related jobs such as a chaplaincy, pastoring or as an evangelist. Prophets also flourish as project managers, sports referees, meeting facilitators and decision analysts since bringing order is part of their spiritual job description. Scribal prophets excel when working in the court system and police departments. Prophets with a healing mantle work well in the healthcare industry. The creatives flourish as teachers and in the entertainment industry. As a caveat, the prophetic personality gone wrong can produce tyrannical leaders as well as those who develop cult followings.

The INFJ personality type has produced great leaders like Jesus, Martin Luther King, Jr., Nelson Mandela, and Mahatma Gandhi. The dark side of this personality shaped twisted leaders like Adolf Hitler, David Koresh, and Osama bin Laden. Some of the creatives with this personality type include Oprah Winfrey, Jamie Foxx, Lady GaGa, Nicole Kidman, Adam Sandler, Prince, Tom Selleck and Al Pacino. World leaders and philosophers include Mother Teresa, Aristophanes, Calvin Coolidge, Thomas Jefferson and Woodrow Wilson.

30

WITCHES IN THE WORKPLACE

The spirit of Jezebel has taken over the workplace. According, to a study conducted at Kaiser Permanente, 88 percent of all people had either seen workplace bullying or had been a victim of it. Workplace bullying has become a staple today.

So often, prophets can be the target of these vicious assaults. I base my previous statement on my own experience as well as speaking with other workplace prophets. Prophets tend to wear the bull's eye because they are not comfortable with the status quo and tend to challenge the system and processes.

Toward the end of my marketplace career, I focused my energy on process improvement. Although I was hired to do exactly that, taking action did not go over well with my bosses. Instead, my suggestions for improvement only served to create endless angst and the powers that be wanted me gone—just like I knew it was time for me to go. The tactics utilized to remove me were far less than ethical. Their agenda was "by any means necessary," but I understood that what God had given me could not be taken away from me. I would be removed when God was done with me there.

The primary battle stance to take in dealing with a person who has the spirit of Jezebel is not to take the attack personally. The issue is more about their insecurities than it is about you. Either you intimidate them, or they fear you will outdo or expose them. They struggle with deep-seated identity issues like envy and jealousy. They are afraid of you and the One who lives inside of you. You must also recognize that you are encroaching on enemy territory.

The last department in which I worked for my company was known for its tyrannical leadership and guerrilla tactics. Certain characteristics identify a workplace witch. The following list contains the primary signs that indicate Jezebel's demonic assault:

- o They are very manipulative.

- They railroad all conversations because their objective is to create confusion. Nothing they say is valid.

- They are often very critical of and demean their subordinates.

- They seek to invalidate people and shake their confidence.

- They are sticklers for detail, they easily recognize others' mistakes and hide their own.

- Initially, they are very cordial as they size up people looking for any weakness on which they can capitalize.

- Everything they do is driven by selfish ambition.

No one is helpless in this situation, and no one should accept abuse. Recognizing the need for an effective battle strategy is vital. Spiritual warfare is part of every believer's daily agenda as much as attending a meeting, responding to emails, taking a conference call or watching a webinar. If God placed you there, no one has the authority to displace you. Pray for your boss and look for another position if God so leads. Oftentimes, God will ask you to stay because He has a bigger plan.

You also have the right to protect yourself and do not allow the intimidation to keep you silent. Report your boss' behavior to your company's compliance department and/or human resources. I let the enemy torment me with silence for a long time. Also, use the ministry of documentation. Archive all email conversations. Use email as opposed to having phone conversations and document every conversation.

The following are four keys to taking an effective battle stance in the workplace:

PRACTICAL PROPHETIC LIVING

1. Before going to work, spend time in prayer and strengthen yourself in the Word. Psalm 119:105 says, *"Your word is a lamp to my feet and a light to my path."*

2. Be grateful. Complaining opens you up to the enemy and makes it easy for him to weaken you. 1 Thessalonians 5:18 says, *"In everything give thanks; for this is the will of God in Christ Jesus for you."*

3. Know that God is fighting for you. David cried out to God, *"Plead my cause, O LORD, with those who strive with me; fight against those who fight against me"* (Psalm 35:1).

4. Take possession of your workplace. God told Moses in Exodus 3:5 (KJV), *"Put off thy shoes from off thy feet: for the place where thou standest is holy ground."* God said to me a long time ago, "Even if you stand amid devils, the ground where your feet touch is holy and restricts demonic activity."

31

A COMPANY OF PROPHETS

The story of Hannah, the barren woman who cried out to God for a child is a familiar passage to many. God answered her request, and, in turn, she vowed to God that the child would belong to Him. *"She said to her husband, "After the boy is weaned, I will take him and present him before the LORD, and he will live there always"* (1 Samuel 1:22). Samuel was committed to the care of Eli the priest as Hannah had promised.

Eli provided for him and cultivated his gift. Most importantly, Eli taught Samuel how to recognize and respond to the voice of the Lord.

> *Therefore, Eli said to Samuel, "Go, lie down; and it shall be, if He calls you, that you must say, 'Speak, LORD, for Your servant hears.'" So, Samuel went and lay down in his place. Now the LORD came and stood and called as at other times, "Samuel! Samuel!" And Samuel answered, "Speak, for Your servant hears"* (1 Samuel 3:9 and 10).

Samuel was God's prophet. 1 Samuel 3:19 and 20 confirm God's call: *"So Samuel grew, and the LORD was with him and let none of his words fall to the ground. And all Israel from Dan to Beersheba knew that Samuel had been established as a prophet of the LORD."* Samuel anointed kings (1 Samuel 10:25, 1 Samuel 16:1), served as Israel's last judge (1 Samuel 7:15), gathered the prophets and ushered in a new prophetic order (1 Samuel 19:20). Because of his relationship with Eli, Samuel understood the value of mentorship, which could have been the catalyst for gathering the prophets and pouring his spirit into them. According to Tim Bartee, the Christian education director of the Church of God, Mountain Assembly:

> There are references to prophets before Samuel, but they are rare and very narrow in their scope. It is after Samuel's life that we see the ministry of the prophet bloom and become the spiritual influence in the nation's history.

PRACTICAL PROPHETIC LIVING

The Biblical text is very clear that prophets traveled in companies or bands. These prophets banded together in numbers to serve the Lord; they were not a ragtag group but a battalion of prophetic power. During the reign of Jezebel, Obadiah protected 100 prophets, so they could continue their ministry and not be slaughtered during the queen's killing spree (1 Kings 18:4). 2 Kings 2:15 and 16 states 50 prophets strong were positioned to aid Elisha in ministry.

The scriptures indicate that the prophets lived together. David and Samuel frequently traveled to Naioth in Ramah according to 1 Samuel 19:22, which says, *"Then he also went to Ramah, and came to the great well that is at Sechu. So, he asked, and said, 'Where are Samuel and David?' And someone said, 'Indeed they are at Naioth in Ramah.'"* Also in 1 Samuel 19:19, *"Now it was told Saul, saying, 'Take note, David is at Naioth in Ramah!'"* David understood the spiritual authority that rested on a prophetic house. The word *Naioth* comes from the Hebrew word *Navith*, which is translated to mean "an abode of prophets." The Complete Jewish Bible translates *Naioth* as "dormitory."

During Samuel's tenure, the prophets were referred to as a "company" who appeared together in Gilgal and Ramah. In Elijah and Elisha's day, they were referred to as "the sons of the prophets" who gathered in Gilgal (2 Kings 4:38), Jericho and Bethel. In Acts 13:1, they gathered at the church in Antioch. These men and women were linked for a specific purpose and collectively worked together. Like animals stay close to their pack and understand the strength in numbers, so must the prophets. God used these groups of prophets to confirm Saul's anointing (1 Samuel 10:2) and to witness and confirm the transfer of mantles from Elijah to Elisha (2 Kings 2:15). They were instrumental in the anointing of King Jehu (2 Kings 9:1). They helped rebuild the house of God in Jerusalem (Ezra 5:2). They cared for their own (2 Kings 4:1).

2 Kings 4:1 demonstrates the significance and benefit of the prophetic community. Most of us have heard about the miracle of the widow woman and the jar of oil, but what is more important is the catalyst for that miracle. The passage reads as follows:

PRACTICAL PROPHETIC LIVING

A certain woman of the wives of the sons of the prophets cried out to Elisha, saying, "Your servant my husband is dead, and you know that your servant feared the LORD. *And the creditor is coming to take my two sons to be his slaves.*

This passage exudes the power of a prophetic company. Elisha did not look for this woman; she cried out to him, and he responded to her based-on relationship.

Prophets naturally gravitate toward the prophetic community. I started realizing that every person who came to me for mentoring or counseling had a prophetic gift. As a believer, every church that I have attended had a prophetic thrust. It is important for prophets, especially young and inexperienced ones, to gather together for training and fortification in a *healthy* community. I want to reiterate that no one can train a person to be a prophet; he is born one (Jeremiah 1:5).

The core of prophetic training is nurturing the call that is already present. Like any gift, you need training. The prophetic gift is so powerful that it could be a weapon of mass destruction if you are not taught how to utilize it properly. If you are not taught how to govern the environment around you, great emotional and spiritual damage can occur to you and others. Another purpose of a prophetic company is for the protection of their young. Like any predatory animal will attempt to seize young and defenseless cubs. Likewise, the enemy will also try to hinder and even put an end to a young prophet's future ministry. The spirit of Herod roams through the earth, trying to cut-off the prophet's voice prematurely. That is why it is important to continue the academic and spiritual training of prophets with the one goal being maturation.

Satan is always trying to mimic the work of God in the earth to create deception. I have included as a reference, the scriptures that refer to false prophets. Just like God's prophets gather together, so do false prophets convene. The following are scripture references validating that fact; (1 Kings 18:19, 40; 1 Kings 22:6; 2 Chronicles 18:5; 1 Kings 22:10; 2 Chronicles 18:9; 1 Kings 22:12-14; 2 Chronicles 18:11-13; 1 Kings 22:19-23; 2 Chronicles 18:18-22; Nehemiah 6:14).

32

OPERATING IN PROPHETIC PRECISION

A prophet must operate as a military sniper. They must abide in the secret place, be accurate, be able to identify the enemy and fire at long range. Operating in prophetic precision minimizes friendly fire and is a requirement for a skilled and mature prophet.

1 Kings Chapters 13:1-25 are an outline of prophetic accuracy. *Bethel,* meaning "the house of God," was the resting place of the altars built by Abraham (Genesis 7:8) and Jacob (Genesis 28:18). At the division of the kingdoms, Bethel became known, under the leadership of Jeroboam, for its corrupt priesthood. It was located roughly ten miles north of Judah, the capital city of Jerusalem. The following elements are the keys to prophetic precision.

The Prophet Promptly Obeys the Voice of the Holy Spirit

Upon hearing the word of the Lord, an unnamed prophet came to Bethel. He entered the temple when Jeroboam was conducting his priestly duties by offering up incense. The man of God gave no sign of resistance or hesitancy to God's directives. I Kings 13:1 says, *"And behold, a man of God went from Judah to Bethel by the word of the Lord, and Jeroboam stood by the altar to burn incense."*

The Prophet Speaks the Word as Given and as Directed

The man of God did not address Jeroboam. His instructions from the Lord was to speak directly to the altar, and he did as he was commanded.

> *Then he cried out against the altar by the word of the Lord, and said, "O altar, altar! Thus, says the LORD: 'Behold, a child, Josiah by name, shall be born to the house of David; and on you, he shall sacrifice the priests of the high places who burn incense on you, and men's bones shall be burned on you.*

PRACTICAL PROPHETIC LIVING

The Prophet Understands Prophetic Timing

The word of the Lord is specific to prophetic timing. The prophet came, and he spoke. When God is not speaking, the prophet is silent (I Kings 13:1). When God is speaking, the prophet opens his mouth in bold declaration. Everything you hear or see is not to be declared at that moment. It is important that the mature prophet seeks God for timing. A word spoken out of season can bring more harm than good, especially if the Holy Spirit has not yet dealt with that person. Proverbs 25:11, 12 says, *"A word fitly spoken is like apples of gold in settings of silver. Like an earring of gold and an ornament of fine gold is a wise rebuker to an obedient ear."* As addressed in previous chapters, New Testament prophets often confirm what the Holy Spirit has already spoken to someone. The Holy Spirit spoke to me and said, "You cannot change a person if he has not first heard my voice." True prophets bring understanding and teach; they do not mesmerize or confuse.

The Prophet Understands the Difference Between Spiritual and Natural Authority

Jeroboam was obviously the king but, at that moment, the prophet overrode his natural authority. There are times when God will have His prophet speak to people in authority although he does not hold a position.

I have had many encounters when God used my relationship with a leader to bring correction. The caveat is that this correction must be done from a position of respect and honor because we are to obey those who have rule over us. Romans 13:1 (NLT), *"Everyone must submit to governing authorities. For all authority comes from God, and those in positions of authority have been placed there by God."* The other forewarning to consider is that God is always after divine order and His plans take precedence over the plans of men.

PRACTICAL PROPHETIC LIVING

The Prophetic Anointing Will Always Confront False Worship

The prophetic anointing abrogates false worship systems and idolatry. In John 4:23, the prophet Jesus confronted the woman at the well concerning her theology of worship. He declared to her, *"But the hour is coming, and now is, when the true worshipers will worship the Father in spirit and truth; for the Father is seeking such to worship Him."*
1 Kings 12:32-33 documents the elaborate worship structure Jeroboam had instituted.

> *Jeroboam ordained a feast on the fifteenth day of the eighth month, like the feast that was in Judah, and offered sacrifices on the altar. So, he did at Bethel, sacrificing to the calves that he had made. And at Bethel he installed the priests of the high places which he had made. So, he made offerings on the altar which he had made at Bethel on the fifteenth day of the eighth month, in the month which he had devised in his own heart. And he ordained a feast for the children of Israel, and offered sacrifices on the altar and burned incense.*

Interestingly, in 1 Kings 13:2-9, God did not directly speak to Jeroboam's sin at that moment but spoke directly to the object of His affection. He cursed the altar, which represented the entire system of worship.

The Prophet Understands That God Always Has a Plan

Even as this nation's systems decline, and society shuns the true and living God, He always has a plan. Debauchery and false worship have been a part of the world system for as long as it has been in existence. A prophet of God can never be discouraged by the condition of society. He cannot allow his message to be altered by the clear majority because God's plan of redemption is always in motion. As Jeroboam was offering his sacrifices on the altar, God was already one step ahead of the king. The providence and foreknowledge of God were establishing His will and future lineage. The man of God began to declare in 1 Kings 13:2, *"Behold, a child, Josiah by name, shall be born to the house of David; and on you he shall sacrifice the priests of the high places who burn incense on you, and men's bones shall be burned on you."*

The Prophet Knows God Will Always Confirm His Word

The man of God declared that God would confirm His word by a sign. Right after He had declared the word, the altar was split in two; the ashes poured on the ground. If we are declaring the word of the Lord, the Holy Spirit will always confirm His word. Mark 16:20 says, *"And they went out and preached everywhere, the Lord working with them and confirming the word through the accompanying signs. Amen."* The word "them" in the original text is italicized, which means that the word was added by the translators to bring clarity. Therefore, removing the word "them" confirms that God did not work with the disciples; He worked with His word.

The Prophet Must Operate in Love

Jeroboam was incensed at the man of God's bold declaration and sought him arrested. As Jeroboam extended his hand toward the prophet, it immediately withered. But out of the bowels of God's mercy and the plea of Jeroboam, his hand was restored to normal at the word of the man of God. Regardless of the weight of our message, we have a moral obligation to pray for people. The results and outcomes are up to God—not us.

The Prophet Understands God's Divine Protection

Jeroboam's attempt to harm the prophet was to no avail. God quickly stepped in and thwarted him because God will always protect His prophets. One of the enemy's deadliest tactics to use against a prophet is fear. After Elijah's greatest victory, he fled in terror from the threat of Jezebel.

1 Kings 19:1-3, *And Ahab told Jezebel all that Elijah had done, also how he had executed all the prophets with the sword. Then Jezebel sent a messenger*

to Elijah, saying, "So let the gods do to me, and more also, if I do not make your life as the life of one of them by tomorrow about this time." And when he saw that, he arose and ran for his life, and went to Beersheba, which belongs to Judah, and left his servant there.

1 Kings 13:4 exemplifies God's divine protection over His messenger. As Jeroboam extended his hand to apprehend the prophet, God conclusively intervened.

The Prophet Obeys God's Divine Instructions

This is discussed in-depth in a previous chapter, but I want to reinforce this principle in the present chapter. God's prophets cannot be bought. After his hand had been healed, Jeroboam extended an invitation to the man of God. *"Then the king said to the man of God, "Come home with me and refresh yourself, and I will give you a reward"* However, the man of God boldly responded to the king:

If you were to give me half your house, I would not go in with you; nor would I eat bread nor drink water in this place. For so it was commanded me by the word of the LORD, *saying, 'You shall not eat bread, nor drink water, nor return by the same way you came' (1 Kings 13:8-9).*

The ministry of the prophet should be far more important than what we can acquire. I am not opposed to honorariums, and I do believe they are in order, but if God commands you to minister without compensation, then He has the final say.

Guard Yourself After a Victory

God commanded the man of God not to eat or drink with anyone (1 Kings 13:9). A prophet's senses can be slightly altered because of the amount of spiritual fortitude and physical energy it takes to work prophetically. Despite this, God will not deviate from His instructions to His prophet. The man of God obeyed the first solicitation, but he ignored the second one. After he stood his ground against Jeroboam, the old prophet's sons pursued him. The enemy is relentless and will pursue you from every angle.

Beware of False Prophets

After the sons of the old prophet pursued the man of God and identified his whereabouts, the old prophet approached him and proceeded to tell him a boldfaced lie: *"I too am a prophet as you are, and an angel spoke to me by the word of the LORD, saying, 'Bring him back with you to your house, that he may eat bread and drink water'"* (1Kings 13:18).

Initially, there is a drastic delineation between the phrases "man of God" and "I am a prophet." The man of God neither announced his arrival nor did he confirm his credentials. As a prophet of God, self-proclamation is unnecessary. The Bible says Samuel was known from Dan to Beersheba—without the auspices of the Internet, television or radio. Matthew 7:22 says, *"Many will say to Me in that day, 'Lord, Lord, have we not prophesied in Your name, cast out demons in Your name, and done many wonders in Your name?'"*

For a prophet to plummet into discouragement and depression following an assignment is very common. We now know that the prophetic ministry can be lonely, and more than likely, the man of God was sent to a region where he was unknown. The fact that the old prophet recognized his call and offered a sense of camaraderie could be the reason why the man of God allowed himself to be deceived by this invitation.

Additionally, the old prophet declared that an angel had spoken to him and not God Himself. God knows how to communicate with His servants clearly. Paul wrote in Galatians 1:8, *"But even if we, or an angel from heaven, preach any other gospel to you than what we have preached to you, let him be accursed."*

It is not clear why the old prophet was interested in this young man, and it will not always be clear why people are interested in you. Many times, jealousy and envy are at the root. The old prophet was already present in Bethel, but God had to send someone all the way from Judah to get the job done. Most likely, this prophet had accepted the social order of the day and did not oppose the established worship system. He probably questioned why God had used the man of God instead of him.

God Will Judge His Prophets

God's judgment prevails when it comes to His prophets. The man of God lost his life for disobeying God. The old prophet was not corrected. The Spirit of the Lord apprehended the old prophet and prophesied the man of God's demise. God used an unlikely vessel to correct the man of God; He will use whomever he chooses.

But you came back, ate bread, and drank water in the place of which the LORD *said to you, "Eat no bread and drink no water," your corpse shall not come to the tomb of your fathers. So, it was, after he had eaten bread and after he had drunk, that he saddled the donkey for him, the prophet whom he had brought back. When he was gone, a lion met him on the road and killed him. And his corpse was thrown on the road, and the donkey stood by it. The lion also stood by the corpse* (1 Kings 13:22).

33

ESTABLISHING A PROPHETIC MINISTRY

All ministries require structure, and establishing any ministry takes capable laborers and a qualified leader. We should never be in the practice of hiring people simply because they *say* they are Christians. Analyzing their lives, their last ministry assignments and their spiritual health is a must. In the prophetic ministry, I believe it is critical to properly train those who will serve in any capacity in your ministry. Never hire people because you are desperate or because they have gifts. I would much rather do the work all by myself than hire the wrong person.

Since part of the prophetic personality is wired to fix dead and broken things, it is important that you avoid hiring ministry projects. A ministry project is an individual who may be skilled but is not healed. They will take more than they will ever give and will use the ministry to give them relief rather than advance God's kingdom. You will spend more time ministering to them than you will giving them responsibility.

The author, Dr. Paula Price, said, "Beware of people who come in over serving and over giving. They are the ones whose motives are not pure. By the time you recognize them; the damage has already been done."

A Pastor gave the account of hiring a woman who was very gifted and extremely well-known in their region. He said, his one mistake was not verifying her last ministry assignment. She did more damage to his ministry than they ever anticipated; by the time they recognized it, it was too late.

Another aspect of building a sound ministry structure is having the ability to delegate. If you are a person of excellence, delegation can be difficult for you. It is like giving your baby to a stranger. When you choose the right people, God will grace them with the ability to get things done, and your spirit will be upon them.

Moses was a faithful servant and diligently served God's people. He gave them godly counsel, helped them sort out their difficult issues and taught them the word of the Lord. Exodus 18:14 says they stood before Moses from morning until evening. Jethro, Moses' father-in-law, corrected Moses and instructed him to delegate his duties so that he would be able to endure. Exodus 18:21 and 22 says,

Moreover, you shall select from all the people able men, such as fear God, men of truth, hating covetousness; and place such over them to be rulers of thousands, rulers of hundreds, rulers of fifties, and rulers of tens. And let them judge the people at all times. Then it will be that every great matter they shall bring to you, but every small matter they themselves shall judge. So, it will be easier for you, for they will bear the burden with you.

When we do not exercise our ability to delegate, we can wear ourselves out and diminish the longevity of our ministry.

34

PROPHETIC DREAMS AND VISIONS

The Bible confirms that God speaks to us in dreams. Saul inquired of the Lord because the Philistine army struck fear in his heart, and he needed a battle strategy quick! The passage records, *"When Saul saw the army of the Philistines, he was afraid, and his heart trembled greatly. And when Saul inquired of the LORD, the LORD did not answer him, either by dreams or by Urim"* (1 Samuel 28:5, 6).

We also learned in a previous chapter that they are one of a prophet's initial encounters with God based on Numbers 12:6, which says, *"Hear now My words: If there is a prophet among you, I, the LORD, make Myself known to him in a vision; I speak to him in a dream."* Dreams and visions are the languages of the spirit and are given for different purposes. Dreams often require interpretation but by some accounts, can be literal. A dream happens while you are asleep or in an unconscious state, and a vision happens while you are awake. Most often, dreams serve as divine warnings and instructions, either for an individual or a group of persons.

For example, in one of my conferences, I was praying for a woman who had a dream her mother was killed in a car accident. Regrettably, that woman's mother died exactly as she saw it in her dream. This fulfillment of her dream was very painful both spiritually and emotionally for the young lady. She carried the pain, grief, and guilt for years.

I believe if someone had been available to provide prophetic direction, she would have been able to process the situation more easily. I am not inferring she would have been able to prevent what happened, but with prophetic guidance, perhaps, she could have made some sense of the event. Maybe, she would have been better prepared to deal with the tragic loss of her mother.

Sometimes, God reveals events that we cannot change, but He is affording us the time to make the necessary natural, spiritual, and emotional preparations to address those situations. The prophet Agabus (Acts 21:11) declared Paul's fate to him, and Paul could do nothing to stop the ensuing events. At other times, we have the authority to pray and alter the outcome.

Dreams and visions are not merely random communications, and for the prophet, they are vivid, brilliant and etched in the spirit. John the Baptist's destiny was altered by his father having a vision.

> *But behold, you will be mute and not able to speak until the day these things take place, because you did not believe my words which will be fulfilled in their own time." And the people waited for Zacharias, and marveled that he lingered so long in the temple. But when he came out, he could not speak to them; and they perceived that he had seen a vision in the temple, for he beckoned to them and remained speechless* (Luke 1:20-22),

Jesus' life was preserved by a dream, which is chronicled in Matthew 2:22 and 23. God warned Jesus' earthly father, Joseph, in a dream not to go to Judea but instead to Nazareth, *"And being warned by God in a dream; he turned aside into the region of Galilee"* (v. 22).

Paul received ministry directives in a vision. Acts 16:9, *"And a vision appeared to Paul in the night. A man of Macedonia stood and pleaded with him, saying, "Come over to Macedonia and help us."* These biblical accounts tell us merely that dreams and visions are specific modes of communications that require validation through the scriptures. If your dreams are showing you things that violate the Word of God then most likely, there is some element of demonic intrusion.

Demonically influenced dreams are very disjointed and paralyzing. They are the catalyst for nightmares, night tremors and sleep hysteria. When my daughter was attending college at Oral Robert's University, she began experiencing episodes of sleep paralysis—being in a semi-conscious state but unable to move. While she was in these states, she reportedly heard voices; animals, and eerie, demonic-sounding noises. As she declared the blood of Jesus over her life, these episodes would cease.

I believe what my daughter encountered were periods of demonic assaults as a person is the most vulnerable while asleep. Since she has been home, these episodes have subsided. I have talked to many prophets who have shared the same experiences. If God uses dreams and visions as a mode of communication, the enemy will also attempt to short circuit and obstruct a person's synapses.

I dream quite frequently, but as I have gotten older, and more disciplined in hearing the spirit, they have decreased. However, during times of heavy spiritual warfare, they increase. Some prophets dream infrequently; some see visions more than they dream. The language of the spirit can vary and is based on the individual. For this reason alone, it is important to understand how God speaks to you. I make a point of journaling my dreams as I have found revelation from them is progressively revealed. I have received key, life-altering instructions and information through dreams.

Recording your dreams so that information is not lost in translation is important. Then seek the guidance of the Holy Spirit for the interpretation. Often, the interpretation is not immediate but may require a little more concentrated time with the Holy Spirit for clarity. On a few occasions, it has taken years for me to fully understand some of the messages that God has spoken to me in dreams and visions. Even through the years, I can remember almost every detail; they remain as vivid as they were the day that I had them. A prophet should take his dreams and visions seriously.

Although dreams and visions are one of the primary ways that God speaks to His prophets, He is not limited to speaking to man in this manner. *"For God may speak in one way, or in another, in a dream, in a vision of the night, when deep sleep falls upon men, while slumbering on their beds"* (Job 33:14-15). Also, because a person has dreams and visions, it does not necessarily indicate he is a prophet. I have discovered that what separates divine messages from normal dreams and visions is a prophet's frequent spiritual encounters and having significant recall about the details.

I want to reiterate that a prophet's dreams and visions are significant and are an important part of his assignment. Amos 3:7 (NIV) says, *"Surely the Sovereign LORD does nothing without revealing his plan to his servants the prophets."*

PART TWO

HEALING THE WOUNDS

"So, Moses did as the Lord commanded him. And the congregation was gathered together at the door of the tabernacle of meeting. And Moses said to the congregation, "This is what the Lord commanded to be done." Then Moses brought Aaron and his sons and washed them with water" (Leviticus 8:4-6).

35

THE WOUND PRINCIPLE

My professional opinion is that a prophet needs to walk in an unprecedented level of healing more than any other gifting in the Bible. The prophet's ministry tends to be very dynamic and can quickly draw people as no other ministry function can. The prophetic church in which I was trained grew from a few hundred people to over 10,000 in a little under three years. The ministry was dynamic, and people's lives were significantly altered by the Holy Spirit dispensing His ministry through the prophet.

On the opposite side of the coin, if the prophet is not healed, tremendous damage can be done to God's people. Therefore, understanding the "wound principle" is critical because a wounded prophet mounting the pulpit is dangerous.

A wounded prophet tends to lust after the adoration and attention he receives from men, and unfortunately, he must manipulate people to keep it. Wounded prophets are so afraid of losing their notoriety that they often refuse correction.

When gaining momentum in ministry, be mindful that healing in one area of your life does not constitute healing in every area of your life. Recognize that every wound should be addressed individually.

The wound principle states that scars qualify you, and wounds disqualify you. Scars are sites of healing, whereas open wounds have the propensity to be hotbeds of infection. Spiritual wounds can be compared to natural wounds in the sense that those wounds that are left untreated are always susceptible to infection, which can spread and cause damage to the surrounding tissue.

No matter the source of the wound, if it is not identified and controlled, the opportunity is there to injure those around us. Wounds can take several months to heal, so be patient with God and yourself. Medically, depending on the depth of the wound, the last stage of healing can take up to two years. If you have been dealing with rejection since you were five years of age, the pain will not go away overnight. If you continue to follow the instructions of those in your

HEALING THE WOUNDS

leadership circle and the instructions of the Holy Spirit, soon, your wound will no longer manage your life. You will gradually gain the skills and the tools to manage it, rather than use ministry to fill the void.

One of the most harmful actions you can take as you heal is to suppress your emotions so that you do not have to feel the pain. As you are reading this book, the Holy Spirit (John 14:26) is granting you the strength and comfort you need. Even though you may deal with some issues for a lifetime, the goal is for you to control the weakness; the weakness will no longer control you.

Paul, the apostle, was given a thorn in his flesh that God refused to remove. However, God's grace was sufficient for Paul to be able to manage that issue effectively and not allow it to hinder his ministry (2 Corinthians 12:8, 9). As relentless as the enemy is with perverting and marring your image, be as relentless with taking on the image of Christ!

Acknowledging and owning a weakness can be very difficult. As a prophet of God, your sight must be far-reaching, and you must be more concerned about the body of Christ than you are about your reputation. Naaman, a highly respected and revered, valiant warrior, was the commander of King Aram's army. Through Naaman's tenure, the Lord gave Aram victory, but there was one problem: Naaman was a leper; he had a wound.

In Bible days, leprosy or Hansen's disease, which will be discussed in a later chapter in depth, was considered to be a highly contagious and debilitating disease, which devastated and disfigured its victims. When faced with his opportunity for healing, Naaman responded with a spirit of pride, disobedience, and anger (2 Kings 5:9-11). He was offended by the prophet's instructions. God's directive is not contingent on a person's comfort or availability but on His sovereignty and man's obedience.

At that time in his life, Naaman was advancing and experiencing great success and felt that the word of the Lord concerning his healing was too onerous. He felt as if the prophet Elisha should have taken a shortcut to save him the trouble. From this story, a person must learn to accept that obedience and humility are the catalysts to total healing. Naaman was instructed by the prophet to wash only in the Jordan and to dip seven times. Nothing else would have produced God's desired results.

The original intent of some men and women of God is not to harm the body of Christ; their primary issue is not deception but ignorance about the strategy of the enemy. Acknowledge the fact that the enemy is very patient; he will allow you to advance while he strategically plans an attack on an area of weakness. Be encouraged that once you identify these areas, God will take up your cause according to Philippians 1:6 (NIV), *"Being confident of this, that he who began a good work in you will carry it on to completion until the day of Christ Jesus."* The wounds of rejection, shame, abuse, neglect, addiction, fornication, adultery, abandonment, pornography, bitterness, lack of forgiveness and fear are slowly eating away at the moral fiber of the prophets and hindering the effectiveness of the body.

One of the primary ways infection spreads, in the natural, is by a person ingesting contaminated food or water. It is both delusional and reckless to think that what is done off the pulpit has no bearing on what is disseminated and inseminated over and into the people of God. A *pandemic* is "an epidemic of infectious disease across a vast geographical area." The church's spiritual pandemic is virtually being ignored by the masses because they are so heavily intoxicated by prophets who are infected and impotent.

These wounded prophets are now caught in a perpetual cycle that is difficult to escape from, and the fear of losing it all is paralyzing. Jesus said, *"What good is it for someone to gain the whole world, yet forfeit their soul?"* (Matthew 8:36, NIV). Regrettably, some are harboring these spiritual fugitives, sustaining the spread of infectious diseases, which is evidence that the church is rotting to the core. A biblical principle is to restore fallen leaders, but that restoration is strongly contingent on the nature of the sin, the frequency of the sin, and the individual's willingness to change and get help. Hebrews 6:4 (ISV) states, *"For it is impossible to keep on restoring to repentance time and again people who have once been enlightened, who have tasted the heavenly gift, who have become partners with the Holy Spirit."*

HEALING THE WOUNDS

In my experience, the rapidity in which a person heals is directly related to how much they love God apart from ministry. Many love God because of what He can do and has done rather than for who He is. Moses refused to take a step further unless God went with Him. Moses told God, *"If Your Presence does not go with us, do not bring us up from here"* (Exodus 33:15).

If reinstallation is an option, rigorous and exhaustive therapy and restorative care are imperative. A wound can stop bleeding in a few days, but that does not mean the injury is healed on the inside. Even considering all the human care, restoration to ministry is only up to the sovereignty of God. David was restored as a man after God's own heart; Eli and his entire lineage were cut off. God alone knows the condition of the heart and the true nature of the sin. He only restores because He has a greater transcending trans-generational plan.

Prophetic leaders must diligently strive to walk in the similitude of Christ and be examples. The principle reason that Jesus was so powerful on this earth is that the God of this world could find nothing reprehensible in Him (John 14:30). Stopping the hemorrhaging is crucial for this hour! Whole and complete prophets who desire nothing but the things of God—not fame, not fortune, not influence, not power, not money—and do not lust after a bride who is not their own must be produced. They are driven by one consuming passion: Christ and His mission alone.

Our hearts must bleed, and our spirits should be passionate with intercession for the innocent people who unknowingly get caught in the crossfire. Certainly, not all the responsibility is on the prophet because individually, every person is accountable for his walk and spiritual growth. But God said in Jeremiah 3:15 (NIV), *"Then I will give you shepherds after my own heart, who will feed you with knowledge and understanding."* Therefore, it is a spiritual principle that we put our trust in the designated man or woman of God. But because of the rapidity in which ministries are deteriorating, the people of God are becoming more and more disillusioned. The initial reaction to a prophet is suspicion and skepticism, assuming he is counterfeit rather than authentic.

HEALING THE WOUNDS

One of the most overlooked responsibilities of a prophet is intercession. Prophets are ministers of the interior and an undercurrent that has the power and authority to shift the tide. Prophets cover and protect the church and command angelic intervention on its behalf. God spoke to Ezekiel and said, *"And I sought for a man among them, that should make up the hedge, and stand in the gap before me for the land, that I should not destroy it: but I found none"* (Ezekiel 22:30, KJV).

This part of the assignment is not a high-profile position. On many assignments, some will never know a prophet's name or even know that individual was sitting among them, but the impact he has will not be diminished. I believe the prophet lives most of his life in the "cave" and only comes out to report for duty. He must refuse to be caught up in the sensationalism.

Prophet, I command you this day to heal. There is a position in the kingdom organizational chart that is empty and vacant because you are not on your post. A pastor told the story of a man who desired deliverance, wholeness, and freedom from sin, but he was a leper. This man was bound by drug addiction for many years. He would be sober for months and would then fall back into the pattern of addiction. Sin on a cycle is not deliverance. When the man came to the pastor pleading for help, he asked him, "When will I be free?"

The pastor responded, "When your desire to be delivered is greater than your desire to get high."

Prophet, you are the property of and under the employment of Jesus. Paul wrote in Galatians 5:24 (NLT), *"Those who belong to Christ Jesus have nailed the passions and desires of their sinful nature to his cross and crucified them there."* Let the surgery commence.

36

ABANDONED

Josh McDowell said his father told him, "A problem well defined is half solved." In this chapter, we will learn and understand how deep-seeded rejection can enter the life of a prophet. This type of rejection can open the door to severe mental and emotional trauma. It can also be the anchor in which the enemy can legally torment a prophet. Moreover, this kind of rejection goes far beyond the rejection that God uses to train a prophet for ministry.

The wounds of an absent father are undoubtedly the chief perpetrator for abandonment. When a father is absent, it makes it difficult for a person to interact with God. As Christians, we are admonished in the scriptures to receive God as our Father, which can be extremely problematic in these situations. If our natural fathers were physically or emotionally absent or abusive, our perception of a father is skewed.

Abandonment violates man's Kingdom promise. Romans 8:15 says, *"For you did not receive the spirit of bondage again to fear, but you received the Spirit of adoption by whom we cry out,* **'Abba***, Father."* The term Abba implies a dependent and deeply affectionate relationship. He said in Ephesians 1:5 and 6, *"Having predestined us to adoption as sons by Jesus Christ to Himself, according to the good pleasure of His will, to the praise of the glory of His grace, by which He made us accepted in the Beloved."* Additionally, He guaranteed in His Word that He would be a Father to those who did not have fathers and a defender of widows (Psalm 68:5).

As I train and heal prophets, one of the exercises I use is to have a person visualize God as their father to help cultivate a father-child relationship. Following one of those sessions, a young lady said to me, "I can only see God as a molester because that is all I know." For me, God was everything but a provider. I believed, prayed and confessed scripture but never expected my needs to be met because I never expected anything from my natural father. Josh McDowell said, "We project the image of our earthly father on our heavenly father."

HEALING THE WOUNDS

The root issues of abandonment result when the person who is accountable for another person's emotional needs relinquishes his responsibility or fails to provide what his dependents need. Abandonment in full operation produces feelings of deep rejection, loss, grief, worthlessness, anger, and fear. Of abandonment issues, *Psychology Today* reports the following concerning abandonment issues:

> Abandonment experiences and boundary violations are in no way indictments of a child's innate goodness and value. Instead, they reveal the flawed thinking, false beliefs, and impaired behaviors of those who hurt them. Still, the wounds are struck deep in their young hearts and minds, and the very real pain can still be felt today. The causes of emotional injury need to be understood and accepted so they can heal. Until that occurs, the pain will stay with them, becoming a driving force in their adult lives.[19]

Abuse can also be a portal for abandonment since the abuser is emotionally absent and is using its victim to meet their emotional, physical or psychological needs. Abuse can be spiritual, physical, verbal or sexual. Spiritual abuse occurs when a person uses the word of God to inappropriately exact punishment, allegiance or control. This behavior creates a culture of shame, fear and will make a person susceptible to feelings of condemnation. Moreover, when a person is spiritually abused their entire existence is shrouded by the fear of offending God.

Sexual abuse in its severest forms includes, intercourse, molestation, rape, sadism or forced oral copulation. It is important to point out that molestation does not always constitute intercourse. Molestation also happens when a person touches another with sexual intent. Lastly, verbal abuse occurs when an authority figure constantly demeans or attempts to destroy who a person is internally by name calling or undue criticism.

One of my friends, who was a Pediatric Nurse told me about an incident where a three-month old baby was admitted to the hospital for Failure to Thrive. Failure to Thrive or (FTT) is a medical term which indicates a baby's inability to gain weight or inappropriately

HEALING THE WOUNDS

losing weight. After several examinations, it was discovered that the baby's stomach was full of semen. My heart was absolutely crushed. Although the baby will not cognitively remember this incident, damage has already been done to his emotions and soul. Apostle Ron Carpenter said, "The enemy wants to yoke you early." That is why childhood issues more than likely represent the bulk of a person's emotional and spiritual wounds. If Satan can yoke a person early in life, that person can spend most his life trying to heal rather than pursue purpose.

37

TRAUMATIZED

God has no pleasure in seeing His children hurt and He does not use pain or tragedy to teach any of us a lesson. Pastor Creflo Dollar said, "We think heaven is so bankrupt that God has to use the instruments of Hell to teach us a lesson." Additionally, the statement, "time heals all wounds," is simply not true. In fact, the more time elongates, the more debilitated a person becomes and their ability to cope with pain diminishes. Instead of healing, the person becomes increasingly more destructive and self-sabotaging. Frequently, these buried emotions can express themselves in physical diseases and ailments. This behavior can have catastrophic effects on a prophet's ministry.

It cannot be stressed enough that prophets must walk in unprecedented levels of emotional healing. A wounded prophet can exhaust the bulk of their anointing by cleaning up their mistakes rather than advancing the kingdom of God. The church is consistent about teaching the body of Christ how to apprehend destiny and seeking the blessing, but it doesn't adequately teach its members how to process pain or deal with trauma.

While dealing with my emotional trauma and dysfunction, I submitted to the mentorship of another prophet for nearly twelve months. We spoke every day for hours. His final exhortation to me pierced my soul. "If you don't get rid of your limp, everyone you raise up will have the same limp." Assessing your emotional compass is imperative to running a successful and enduring ministry. Knowing how you react, respond and manage traumatic events will help you and the Holy Spirit produce a fruitful work and build a spiritual legacy.

Sometimes people in ministry find great difficulty in comprehending that their issues are affecting people—if their anointing is working. When you see individual lives change, you can become almost immune to your issues. For example, if you are in a church where the leadership struggles with pride, you will see it manifest in many areas throughout their ministry. And often, the leader does not detect the issue or attribute it to their condition. One of the principles of leadership is the duplication of who you are—not what you preach.

At one of the churches to which I was assigned, I worked very closely with the pastor but the closer I got, the more I realized something was desperately wrong. The pastor was traumatized. An event in his past jarred his emotions, fractured his personality and skewed his perception of himself. This trauma opened the door to the ultimate demise of the church. As the ministry began to grow, the foundation became sinking sand, and everything imploded as the pastor's issues began to float to the surface. Sadly, this pastor is no longer in ministry; this is what happens when trauma is not addressed. According to the American Psychological Association,

> Trauma is an emotional response to a terrible event like an accident, rape or natural disaster. Immediately after the event, shock and denial are typical. Longer term reactions include unpredictable emotions, flashbacks, strained relationships and even physical symptoms like headaches or nausea. While these feelings are normal, some people have difficulty moving on with their lives[20]

When a person is traumatized, their emotions are suspended in time. Sometimes, the person's brain protects that individual by blocking off the memory which is why you find trauma victims that simply cannot remember the details. That portion of the tape has seemingly been erased. My mother had a nervous breakdown which deeply affected me and my siblings. I simply cannot remember much of what happened around that time.

Because of trauma people develop what psychologist call coping mechanisms. Coping mechanisms are a person's response to internal or external stress. These mechanisms can take on many shapes and forms, but the consensus of the psychiatric community is the following:

HEALING THE WOUNDS

Introjection

By definition, *introject*[21] is "to incorporate (attitudes or ideas) into one's personality unconsciously." This coping mechanism works well if the parent or guardian was nurturing, loving or supportive. If not, it will have negative effects on a person's identity.

Goodtherapy.org says, "Some mental health professionals believe that introjection is a protective strategy that children employ to cope with unavailable parents, guardians or a traumatic event."[22] Because of this coping mechanism, pain can be turned inward, which can manifest in a person's body as anxiety, depression, fatigue, self-denial, chronic diseases, addiction or self-destructive habits.

Projection

This part of a person's behavioral survival mechanisms defends a person from the outside world and helps him rid himself of unwanted negative feelings. This behavior causes a person to project what he feels on someone else rather than owning the negative emotions. The behavior of people who embrace life as victims is volatile. They attribute all their problems to others by lashing out and being highly critical. Furthermore, they are never able to take responsibility, and it is difficult for them to get ahead in life because their emotions are stuck in past experiences. Instead of dealing with their pain, they inflict pain on those around them.

Addictive Behaviors

According to various psychological viewpoints, addictive behaviors can be physical as well as psychological. When the pain becomes more than these individuals can bear, they turn to habitual behaviors, including recreational drugs, alcohol, gambling, abusive relationships or pornography. These addictive behaviors can also manifest in a person's being a shopaholic or a workaholic; they can even become completely obsessed with their appearance. When it comes to physical appearance, the *Diagnostic and Statistical Manual of*

Mental Disorders (DSM-5) has classified a new obsessive-compulsive disorder called body dysmorphia that makes a person addicted to cosmetic surgery. These habitual behaviors serve to numb the pain, but they also hold their victim's hostage for years.

Codependency:

A clinical definition of *codependency* is "a psychological condition or a relationship in which a person is controlled or manipulated by another who is affected with a pathological condition (as an addiction to alcohol or heroin); *broadly:* dependence on the needs of or control by another."[23] These people, who are dependent on other people are so addicted that they allow the negative behavior to continue. Their codependency manifests itself in being people pleasers; being controlling, possessive, jealous; enablers or rescuers. Codependency can also evidence itself in bitterness and resentment. An addictive personality begins to resent the dependent person because he does not have the capacity to give back what he was given. These people can also be very passive-aggressive when dealing with conflict.

Inner vows, oaths, and agreements

I also want to add inner vows, oaths, and agreements; these are not coping mechanisms but responses. It is a person making verbal agreements, as a child, in reaction to pain or a traumatic event. The purpose of these agreements is to insulate an individual from further damage. These are spiritual contracts that need to be canceled. If they are not canceled, they remain enforced during the life of the contract. What makes these agreements so dangerous is we forget about them. The agreements lie dormant in our souls until an event or a person triggers it. One woman's story is that she vowed a man would never hurt her again. That inner vow catapulted her into a life of homosexuality.

Demonic spirits feed off these covenants because it gives them legal right to enforce them. Numbers 30:2 says, *"If a man makes a vow to the Lord, or swears an oath to bind himself by some agreement, he shall not break his word; he shall do according to all that proceeds out of his mouth."*

Repairing the emotional system and recovering from the pain of life is possible since Jesus said in Matthew 19:26, *"...With men this is impossible, but with God all things are possible."* Job is our example and the perfect case study to show that anyone can heal from a traumatic event. Job recovered from his loss of everything and overcame his grief. Eventually, God restored all his possessions to him (Job 42:16, 17). A person's response to pain determines whether his issues will be a lifelong struggle or a momentary conflict.

The following R's are three practical steps to help deal with emotional pain:

Recognition

The first step is acknowledging and accepting the pain. This step makes pain real and refuses to spiritualize it as an attack of the enemy. Most Christians do not know the difference between the assault of the enemy and a consequence. The bedrock of healing is recognizing that we need help.

After two failed marriages and years of dysfunctional relationships, I finally realized that I needed help. The moment I recognized the need for intervention, my entire life completely changed. In all honesty, my initial call for help was to rescue me from someone else's bad behavior—not me from my own.

Repentance

Secondly, turning from our behavior and changing the way we think about the matter is so important. Satan and his demonic regimes are real and will do everything they can to keep us in a self-imposed prison by distorting our thought patterns. Repentance is also an act of maturity that admits our responsibility. The enemy can initiate a negative cycle, but only we can allow it to perpetuate. I have come to understand that no matter what weapon Satan pulls out of his arsenal, my response will control the outcome. This step is the most crucial because, for most, it is difficult for any person to accede to the fact that his present situation is partly a result of his behavior.

Renouncing

Jesus said in Luke 10:19 (KJV), *"Behold I give unto you power…"* Using your will and the Word of God to disallow these negative emotions the power to operate in your life will transform you from a victim to a victor. Understanding that the enemy only has the power that he is given is so important to renouncing negative emotions.

HEALING THE WOUNDS

38

WHERE THE ENEMY TRAFFICS

Getting hurt is one of life's inevitabilities and learning to process emotional pain is how we release the abundant life that Jesus talked about in John 10:10. A person's inability to do this hinders the gift and call of God on their lives and gives the enemy legal right to traffic. True healing allows us to shut every door where the enemy has access.

As discussed in the previous chapter, many do not understand or have the tools to process painful emotional events but instead develop a myriad of coping mechanisms that mask the pain, never resolving it. Gravitating towards others who constantly need to be rescued is one common way. They are constantly "saving themselves," operating under the guise of "If someone would have done this for me, I would not have experienced the things that I went through."

The problem with this theory is many fail to consider the other person's actions that contributed to their condition. Many times, bondage is a person's cooperating with demonic influences. It is important to remember when ministering to those who are in bondage that often it is a choice since the scriptures declare we are free (John 8:36).

Maslow's *hierarchy of needs*[24] is a motivational theory in psychology comprising a five-tier model of human needs, often depicted as hierarchical levels within a pyramid. His work is significant in helping us understand how the lack of human need can cause emotional deficits. The original hierarchy of needs five-stage model includes:

- **Biological and Physiological needs** - air, food, drink, shelter, warmth, sex, sleep.

- **Safety needs** - protection from elements, security, order, law, stability, freedom from fear.

HEALING THE WOUNDS

- **Love and belongingness needs** - friendship, intimacy, trust, and acceptance, receiving and giving affection and love. Affiliating, being part of a group (family, friends, work).

- **Esteem needs** - achievement, mastery, independence, status, dominance, prestige, self-respect, respect from others.

- **Self-Actualization needs** - realizing personal potential, self-fulfillment, seeking personal growth and peak experiences.

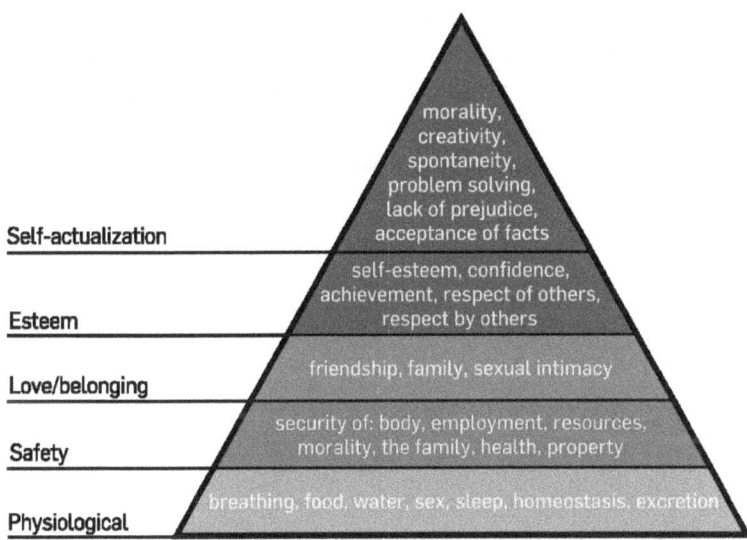

Maslow's theory can help us identify where the enemy can be wreaking havoc in our lives. A breach in any one of these areas can open the door to demonic activity and emotional deficits.

In conclusion, some psychologists say that for a child to mature, he needs to receive acceptance and approval, love and affection, encouragement, security, support, comfort, respect, attention, appreciation, and celebration from his parents. The absence of these intangibles creates a gaping hole that can ultimately destroy a person's life. As you embark out on your own, if these needs are not met, you will spend your entire adult life looking for them. Identifying these vacancies will give you insight into how the enemy can traffic in and out of your life at will.

Scriptures confirm that we have authority over the enemy's assaults. Therefore, he only has the authority to traffic in areas where he has been given permission, consciously or subconsciously. For example, if you grew up with very little affection, you can be more susceptible to sexual sins because of the lack of emotional and physical intimacy. Since the wounds from childhood can be so deeply rooted in your soul, the redeeming work of Holy Spirit is paramount.

In my assessment, I realized that because of being abandoned by my father, my most significant need was security. When I felt, my security was being threatened relationally, financially, spiritually or emotionally, I would panic which created a lot of conflict in my relationships. Once I figured out my trigger, I altered the course of my life and ministry. Prophet, God, wants to heal all your wounds.

HEALING THE WOUNDS

39

EMOTIONAL BARRIERS

The chart below will indicate where the enemy has been allowed to hinder your life. As a guideline, all the areas identified are initiated by the parent, not the child. For example, affection is not when a child goes and hugs a parent it is when the parent lovingly reaches out to the child.

Give each parent a rating of 1 -10. Ten being the best and 0 being the worst. Every area where you scored below 5 gives you a clear indication of a psychological or emotional deficiency. If a parent was absent, addicted or abusive, then the bulk of your answers will be zero's. Also, if your parents excessively argued there will also be areas where you scored low because unresolved conflict in parents creates feelings of abandonment in a child.

This exercise is not created to demean or confront your parent(s); it is only used for identifying deficient needs. Once the need is identified find a promise in God's word that will counteract its effects. If you still have unresolved issues with your parents, letter writing is an effective tool to unleash those negative emotions. It is not necessary to give the letter to your parent(s) unless you feel led by the Holy Spirit.

Emotional Need	Definition	Mother	Father
Acceptance and Approval	Capable or worthy of being accepted. The state of being satisfactory, favorable or adequate.		
Love and Affection	Warm attachment or affection as expressed by a parent to a child. Expressed by physical touch or quality time.		
Encouragement	The act of inspiring or giving hope.		
Security	Safety. Freedom from danger, anxiety or fear.		
Support	To promote the interest or cause. Help or assist.		
Comfort	To strengthen or console in times of grief.		
Respect	To be valued or esteemed.		
Attention	To be noticed or observed.		
Appreciation	The expression of admiration or gratitude.		
Celebration	To honor on special occasions or achievements.		

HEALING THE WOUNDS

40

CHURCH HURT

As addressed in the previous chapter, emotional pain is a part of life and learning to process it is a fundamental skill in the life of a prophet. The prophetic life, more times than not, will be extremely painful and rigorous. Mostly due to the amount of spiritual information, responsibility, and rejection a prophet has to receive and manage. Wounds acquired during childhood have already been addressed; therefore, I would like to focus on wounds that happened while we were serving and advancing the kingdom of God.

At this juncture in the road, it is crucial to settle that ministry is difficult, demanding and draining. In 2 Corinthians 6:4-10, Paul, the apostle, talks about the marks of ministry, which I believe is important for a prophet to understand.

> *But in all things we commend ourselves as ministers of God: in much patience, in tribulations, in needs, in distresses, in stripes, in imprisonments, in tumults, in labors, in sleeplessness, in fastings; by purity, by knowledge, by longsuffering, by kindness, by the Holy Spirit, by sincere love, by the word of truth, by the power of God, by the armor of righteousness on the right hand and on the left, by honor and dishonor, by evil report and good report; as deceivers, and yet true; as unknown, and yet well known; as dying, and behold we live; as chastened, and yet not killed; as sorrowful, yet always rejoicing; as poor, yet making many rich; as having nothing, and yet possessing all things.*

People can be a prophet's greatest asset or his greatest liability. God's Word commands people to co-labor with one another, but for several reasons, working together can be a skill in and of itself. Initially, people are at different levels of maturity, and what one person has overcome can still be a battle for someone else. Secondly, sometimes, people do not serve with the right motives, and their intentions are to create confusion and division to get what they want. Thirdly, jealousy and envy always seem to be an issue in the prophetic community. Lastly, some people simply do not have honorable hearts; that is who they are. Learning to navigate through these personalities is a discipline that requires the wisdom of God.

Many times, when people serve, they tend to absorb hurts and disappointments because, after all, we are working unto the Lord. We also forget that we are human beings and that we have the right to protect ourselves as well as confront those who have offended us (Matthew 18:15-17). The caveat is that when the hurt is at the hands of a leader, a certain protocol must be adhered to or our churches would be imploding from the inside out. Religious rhetoric makes us believe that we do not have the right to confront a leader but that is false.

Church hurt is a true phenomenon; some people recover, and some never do. It was absolutely the grace of God on my life that empowered me to continue in ministry. Everything in me was screaming danger, and my only recourse was to abort the mission. I did not understand why people were responding to me in the way they were. As a young prophet, I made the false assumption that people would be happy to hear what I had to say. I soon realized that the prophetic ministry is the most detested. Prophets were killed, hated, and ostracized. Therefore, it is difficult for me to embrace this newfangled stardom of modern-day prophets. The book of 2 Chronicles Chapter 24 recorded the death of Zechariah after he declared the inspired word of God:

> *Then the Spirit of God came upon Zechariah the son of Jehoiada, the priest, who stood above the people, and said to them, "Thus says God: 'Why do you transgress the commandments of the LORD, so that you cannot prosper? Because you have forsaken the LORD, He also has forsaken you." So, they conspired against him, and at the command of the king, they stoned him with stones in the court of the house of the LORD* (vv. 20, 21).

During this time, I remember going to choir rehearsal at the church I was attending. I was trained to be committed, so I knew I had to go, but every week, anxiety and fear would overtake me. I asked the Lord what was happening, and He said, "You associate going to church with pain." If it were not for a more mature prophet's counsel,

HEALING THE WOUNDS

I would not be in church today. I am giving real-life accounts since this is more than just a book; it is a training manual for future prophetic voices. In the next chapter, we will look, in-depth, at how to manage these ministry wounds.

HEALING THE WOUNDS

41

MANAGING MINISTRY WOUNDS

In ministry, the correct response to hurts and offenses is crucial if you are going to be successful in your endeavors. If you do not respond appropriately, the outcome can damage those who are entrusted to your care and hinder the potency of your ministry. Getting hurt is unavoidable; how you handle those hurts is what matters. If God is stretching you, trust that He knows what is best. If you are being mistreated, trust God will repay what is right. If you moved ahead of the Holy Spirit's voice, know there is forgiveness and a fresh start. People respond to ministry wounds in many ways, but the following areas seem to be the most common:

Pride

The world says the best revenge is success; I say the best revenge is responding in humility. Your response is prideful when you are trying to prove or show people that you are important or have arrived. When this reaction becomes your normal response to being hurt, you run the risk of developing a false personality to cope with pain. Adapting in this manner can be dangerous since authenticity is a ministry requirement.

Lack of Forgiveness

The Bible commands us in Hebrews 12:14-15,

> *Pursue peace with all people, and holiness, without which no one will see the Lord: looking carefully lest anyone fall short of the grace of God; lest any root of bitterness springing up cause trouble, and by this many become defiled.*

If the root of bitterness is not plucked up, it will defile everyone around you. When you refuse to extend the grace and mercy God has

HEALING THE WOUNDS

extended to you, you become callous and cold. I cannot stress enough the importance of knowing that forgiving someone is not contingent on whether the individual acknowledges what they did. When you forgive, you are releasing yourself from the situation and allowing God to handle the matter. Charles Stanley said, "When you refuse to forgive, you are implying Jesus' death on the cross was not enough."

Fear

You become apprehensive about getting back "in the ring," fearing you will be hurt again. You seem unable to bring yourself to take other risks, which can jeopardize future ministry opportunities. If fear is not managed, you can allow yourself to become jaded, disillusioned and stagnant.

Apathy

You don't care anymore; your passion has waned; you have lost your vigor; drive and you have become fainthearted. The enthusiasm you once possessed has turned into disillusionment. You enlist in the army of those who are going through the motions.

Depression

Many times, depression is anger turned inward. You refuse to acknowledge the hurt, which deceives you into believing you are operating by faith. It can also be your response for exacting punishment on yourself from a previous event. Ministry can be painful, and nursing your wounds is imperative. As you make the time to heal, you can frustrate the plans of the enemy.

The Apostle Paul's Response

So, what is the appropriate way to respond to wounds? I believe you can learn a lesson from the Apostle Paul who was the one who

HEALING THE WOUNDS

penned under the inspiration of the Holy Spirit, *"I can do all things through Christ who strengthens me"* (Philippians 4:13).

Acts 14:19-23 highlights one of Paul's first ministry encounters, which ended with an attempt to stone him to death! So how did Paul respond?

- *"And the next day he departed"* (v. 20). He wasted no time apprehending his next assignment.

- *"Preached…and made many disciples"* (v. 21). He didn't withhold the ministry God placed in him.

- *"They returned to Lystra, Iconium, and Antioch"* (v. 21). He returned to the people who stoned him. He did not allow the offense to hinder him.

- *"Strengthening the souls of the disciples"* (v. 21). He was more committed to the mission than his feelings. He encouraged his brothers.

HEALING THE WOUNDS

42

THE WOUNDED PROPHET

In a dream, I had several years ago; I was standing in the back of a church, watching a prophet exit the pulpit after preaching. As he removed his priestly garments, I saw long scars across his shoulders. His face was young, but his body was riddled with knots from old age. I heard the Spirit of God say, "I am grieved, and the prophetic priests are injured." The shoulder scar signified that they were so wounded that they could not carry the ark of the covenant, which represented the presence, power, and provision of God (Hebrews 9:4).

According to *Strong's Concordance* a wound is "a plague [a sudden highly infectious disease]; pestilence [a fatal epidemic disease]; a leprous spot, trauma [a wound caused by sudden physical injury, something that severely jars the mind or emotions]; to be wounded is to profane, defile, or maim." [25] According to *Webster's Dictionary*, a wound [26] is "an injury especially in which the skin is torn, pierced or cut."

As I have already alluded to in previous chapters, you can never minister out of your wounds; you minister from your scars. In the Old Testament, the condition of the priesthood was serious business. Below are God's instructions to Moses.

> *And the Lord spoke to Moses, saying, "Speak to Aaron, saying: 'No man of your descendants in succeeding generations, who has any defect, may approach to offer the bread of his God. For any man who has a defect shall not approach: a man blind or lame, who has a marred face or any limb too long, a man who has a broken foot or broken hand, or is a hunchback or a dwarf, or a man who has a defect in his eye, or eczema or scab, or is a eunuch. No man of the descendants of Aaron, the priest, who has a defect, shall come near to offer the offerings made by fire to the Lord. He has a defect; he shall not come near to offer the bread of his God. He may eat the bread of his God, both the most holy and the holy; only he shall not go near the veil or*

HEALING THE WOUNDS

approach the altar, because he has a defect, lest he profane My sanctuaries; for I the Lord sanctify them (Leviticus 21:16-23).

Then the Lord spoke to Moses, saying, "Speak to Aaron and his sons, that they separate themselves from the holy things of the children of Israel, and that they do not profane My holy name by what they dedicate to Me: I am the Lord. Say to them: Whoever of all your descendants throughout your generations, who goes near the holy things which the children of Israel dedicate to the Lord, while he has uncleanness upon him, that person shall be cut off from My presence: I am the Lord. (Leviticus 22:1-3).

In the Levitical law, priests were held to a higher standard because they were God's public role models for wholeness. Furthermore, these instructions were not given in private but in public so the people they served would know and understand what God's requirements were. There were three conditions identified in the text concerning the priest who ministered bread to the Lord:

- The first group of people were those who had injuries that would heal, such as a broken foot. They would be able to serve once their healing was complete.

- The second group were people who had deformities. They would never be able to minister to the Lord mainly because their condition prohibited them from fully managing their priestly duties. But God provided for these priests and assigned other duties to them as he deemed appropriate.

- The last group of priests were considered unclean due to some type of skin discharge or defect. These priests could not serve until they were healed and their healing was verified. If an unclean priest officiated a sacrificial service, the offering to God would be annulled.

HEALING THE WOUNDS

The current religious climate does not do a good job at vetting pulpiteers. They are merely judged by how quickly they can pack a church or a stadium. The goal is financial more than it is spiritual, and there is very little concern about how they live their private lives. If we believe that the Bible in its totality is by divine inspiration, then we must believe that everything in it is relevant for today. In the Old Testament, people who were wounded (bodily discharges, leprosy, etc.) had to be removed from the general population until they were healed. Jesus bled *for* the people—not *on* the people.

A spiritual wound left unattended can become putrid, multiplying the risk of infecting people and spreading deadly diseases, especially to the weak. A wounded priest's offering an unacceptable sacrifice can devour the body in a matter of hours, and the damage incurred is sometimes not seen for years. Prophets must consider where they are in their healing process. Some are so afraid of losing ground that they will put God's people in jeopardy to keep the ministry growing and the money coming in.

If a person chooses to step back in ministry, it does not mean he cannot recover. In 2016 Megachurch pastor Pete Wilson resigned according to *Charisma Magazine*. His final remark to his congregation was, "And now, more than ever before — I really need your prayers, and I need your support. We've said that this is a church where it's OK to not be okay, and I'm not okay. I'm tired. I'm broken, and I just need some rest." In my opinion, he is to be applauded. His love for God, his people, and the ministry was more important than him maintaining his position as the lead pastor.

Those who refuse to relinquish their pulpits momentarily can continue in ministry, but that does not mean God's hand will be on the work. So many churches continue to operate, but God has stamped *Ichabod*[27] on the front door, and the glory has left the building.

A friend of mine was sharing with me that during a certain season, several pastors committed suicide. As she inquired of the Lord, she was watching a ministry program and saw the pastor's itinerary scrolling across the screen. At that moment, the Holy Spirit said to her, "That is why! They cannot maintain that schedule and stay in My

HEALING THE WOUNDS

presence at the same time." It is imperative that a prophet makes time to heal and be replenished.

Of principal importance are prophetic leaders allowing the Holy Spirit to bind up their wounds and heal them entirely. Prophets must permit God to heal what has been hidden and protected in the inner recesses and depths of their souls. That which the prophet has been unable to face the truth about must be surrendered and exposed. Before taking another step forward, it is pivotal that you go to your place of prayer and get "healed"—lest you continue to minister death to the body. Forward progress does not always mean that you are moving in the right direction!

43

AN ACCEPTABLE SACRIFICE

As discussed in a previous chapter the biblical text contains stringent requirements for the priest of God. Today, so many have etched lives of sin that they erroneously think grace and mercy have lowered the requirements. Because there is no immediate consequence to their sins, they somehow think they are getting away with them. And the more they think they get away with them, the more they gain momentum.

The current temperature of this age is lukewarm. In many churches, the character or lifestyle of the prophets who minister is of very little importance, and the gift seems to be the only deciding factor. In the Old Testament days, a king searched for a prophet to hear the voice of God; today, prophets are called to help raise funds to build up fleshly kingdoms.

A prophet must be careful and discerning about what his assignment is and be sure that he has not been recruited to enter a spiritual bordello. The Lord requires and mandates a twofold sacrificial offering that is acceptable. Those who offer up worship to God must be pure, and the sacrifice should be free from defect or blemish. God's requirements on the acceptability of a sacrifice were stringent. His instructions to Moses were recorded in Leviticus 22:17-25 (AMP),

> *Then the Lord spoke to Moses, saying, "Speak to Aaron and his sons and to all the Israelites and say to them, 'Any man of the house of Israel or any stranger in Israel who presents his offering, whether to fulfill any of their vows or as any of their freewill (voluntary) offerings which they presented to the Lord as a burnt offering—so that you may be accepted—it must be a male without blemish from the cattle, the sheep, or the goats. You shall not offer anything which has a blemish, because it will not be accepted for you. Whoever offers a sacrifice of peace offerings to the Lord to fulfill a special vow to the Lord or as a freewill offering from the herd or from the flock, it must be perfect to be accepted; there shall be no blemish in it. Animals that are blind or fractured or mutilated, or have a sore or a running wound or an itch or scabs, you shall not offer to the Lord nor make an offering of them by fire on*

the altar to the Lord. For a freewill offering you may offer either a bull or a lamb which has an overgrown or stunted member (deformity), but for [the payment of] a vow it will not be accepted. You shall not offer to the Lord any animal which has its testicles bruised or crushed or torn or cut off, or sacrifice it in your land. Nor shall you offer as the food of your God any such [animals obtained] from a foreigner, because their corruption and blemish makes them unfit; there is a defect in them, they shall not be accepted for you.

More than any other gifting, prophets must conduct themselves with absolute integrity. By nature, the prophetic ministry possesses a heightened ability to impact people's lives, which also increases the capacity to cause tremendous harm.

Contritely, give the Lord permission to search your heart and weigh your motives. Psalms 139:23 -24 is David's cry for divine intervention. He said, *"Search me [thoroughly], O God, and know my heart; Test me and know my anxious thoughts; And see if there is any wicked or hurtful way in me, And lead me in the everlasting way"* (AMP). From a pure and cleansed soul, embrace honesty, dare to be transparent and yield to God's correction. Be comfortable with living life under the knife.

HEALING THE WOUNDS

44

KILLING THE ROOT

"And even now the ax is laid to the root of the trees. Therefore, every tree which does not bear good fruit is cut down and thrown into the fire" (Matthew 3:10). The common factor in the rise and fall of prominent ministries is the corruption of the root systems. Once an issue becomes public, it has been brewing under the surface unchallenged for many years, and the correction of God through the prophets has been refused. What you fail to kill will, in the long run, kill you.

Science says that by the time cancer is detected in a person's body, it has been growing for several months and maybe even years. Cancer treatment is not the killing of the roots, but the killing of fruit. Unfortunately, in many cases, by the time cancer is detected, it can be extremely difficult to find the originating source.

The same principle is true with some of these soul issues. Sadly, most people never do the work required to identify the root issues in their lives. Instead, they spend the bulk of their lives plucking fruit rather than destroying roots.

Jesus spoke in parables. He cursed the fig tree and said, *"Let no fruit grow on you ever again." Immediately the fig tree withered away"* (Matthew 21:19). The fig tree withered because the root system was desecrated. Amos 2:9 (NLT) says, *"But as my people watched, I destroyed the Amorites, though they were as tall as cedars and as strong as oaks. I destroyed the fruit on their branches and dug out their roots."*

Webster's Dictionary defines a *root* as "something that functions as a means of anchorage and support. It is an origin or source as relating to a condition or quality." [28] According to Job 18:16, *"His roots are dried out below, and his branch withers above."* Therefore, the divine principle is that killing the root kills the fruit.

Another definition for *root* is "to establish."[29] The enemy works ardently to institute weaknesses in the lives of children long before they ever can fight them off. These compromised areas begin to develop into root systems that will verifiably make them weak in future battles if they go undetected or are ignored. Root systems can become quite intricate and interlock themselves around every aspect of a person's life and being. They can and will asphyxiate the very life out of every relationship and endeavor and encumber the person's forward advancement.

Anything that can hinder a believer's maturity in Christ is considered an adversary. For that reason, Jesus said, *"Agree with your adversary quickly"* (Matthew 5:25). It is essential that the prophet yields to God's cleansing process, especially before he goes into ministry.

These root issues are lying dormant in the hearts and souls of the prophets of God. They can be deceptively operating in them, giving them the impression that they have time to "get it right" before they are exposed. From the pen of the prophet Ezekiel,

> *God asked me, "Son of man, do you see what the leaders of the nation of Israel are doing in secret? Each of them is in the room where his god is, and each one of them is thinking, 'The LORD doesn't see me"* (Ezekiel 8:12, GW).

Once these breaches are manifested, they can cause irreversible damage to the people of God and systematically destroy what took the favor of God, human resources, and years to build. Sadly, some people never recover and completely cut off all communication with the church.

In the life of a prophet, the enemy's one driving aim is to silence his voice of liberty, redemption, and healing. The key to a prophet's healing process is being mindful of the strategies of the enemy. The enemy is patient, relentless, and consistent as illustrated in Luke 4:13, which says, *"Now when the devil had ended every temptation, he departed from Him until an opportune time."* "Opportune time" are the operative words of this verse, which infers that Satan is poised to strike when least expected. *"Be watchful, stand firm in the faith, act like men, be strong"* (1 Corinthians 16:13, ESV).

45

THE WORKS OF THE FLESH

The Apostle Paul wrote in Romans 7:15-17:

> *For what I am doing, I do not understand. For what I will to do, that I do not practice; but what I hate, that I do. If, then, I do what I will not to do, I agree with the law that it is good. But now, it is no longer I who do it, but sin that dwells in me.*

In the book of Galatians 5:16-21, Paul is also addressing the congregation at Galatia regarding the liberty they have been given in Christ, He says,

> *I say then: Walk in the Spirit, and you shall not fulfill the lust of the flesh. For the flesh lusts against the Spirit, and the Spirit against the flesh; and these are contrary to one another, so that you do not do the things that you wish. But if you are led by the Spirit, you are not under the law. Now the **works** of the flesh are evident, which are: adultery, fornication, uncleanness, lewdness, idolatry, sorcery, hatred, contentions, jealousies, outbursts of wrath, selfish ambitions, dissensions, heresies, envy, murders, drunkenness, revelries, and the like; of which I tell you beforehand, just as I also told you in time past, that those who practice such things will not inherit the kingdom of God.*

Clarifying the word "works"[30] is important. According to *Strong's Concordance*, work is "a deed [action] that carries out [completes] an inner desire [intention, purpose]." A prophet cannot be driven by appetite but by destiny. Allowing your flesh to control you diminishes the impact of your message. Living under the scalpel of correction is a necessary discipline that keeps the office pure. The chief end of a prophet is to control your flesh and not let your flesh control you.

One of the most strategic elements of war is to know your enemy. Sun Tzu, a Chinese military strategist, is quoted as saying the following:

HEALING THE WOUNDS

If you know the enemy and know yourself, you need not fear the result of a hundred battles. If you know yourself but not the enemy, for every victory gained you will also suffer a defeat. If you know neither the enemy nor yourself, you will succumb in every battle.[31]

Examine your life and spiritually fortify yourself. We will all fall short and sin as it is the nature of the flesh, but practicing sin is not an option. Many years are needed to train a prophet effectively, and one perpetual proclivity can render the prophet useless to the kingdom of God. One reason the fall of prophets is problematic and at times beyond recovery is because of people's difficulty in even believing that we exist, and our message is by divine inspiration.

One year, I was doing a conference, and I was ministering prophetically to an individual when I motioned to a member of my staff for help; she moved so quickly she startled me. I heard the Holy Spirit say, "Don't ever take advantage of that." As a prophet, I am very careful about how I handle and treat the people of God because I am clear on the fact that they are not *my* servants; they are God's. They are not for my personal use but for the use of the kingdom. I will not allow my fleshly endeavors to profane the kingdom of God.

46

UNCLEAN LIPS

Psalm 141:3 (ESV) is admonishing us to control our mouth gates. It says, *"Set a guard, O LORD, over my **mouth**; keep **watch over** the door of my lips!"* and *"Keep **your** tongue from evil and **your** lips from speaking deceit."* A prophet's greatest asset is his mouth, which can also be his greatest disadvantage. Since prophets' function as God's delegates for divine inspiration, their words carry more impact and weight. More than any other gift, prophets must be careful how they say things to people. Words have power and can live on in the spirit of a person long after we are gone. So many believers think they are hindered by an enemy, when in fact, they are hindered by a word spoken over their lives.

The Holy Spirit taught me years ago about the power of words. He said, "Every word you speak is hanging in the balance waiting to fulfill itself. If it does not fulfill itself, it will make me a liar. If I were a liar, even the very planets themselves would fall out of orbit."

When I was a prophet in training, I felt a person in our leadership group was being manipulated by another member of our church, and that manipulation was agitating my spirit. I was trying so desperately to convince this person that he was falling prey to the enemy's tactics, but my words were not being heeded. The more I pressed, the more he began to resent me. He said to me, "Others can tell me the same thing, but when you tell me, I can't even sleep." Because of that experience, God showed me that a prophetic word out of season could be damaging.

When God called the prophet Isaiah, one of the first concerns Isaiah was faced with was the condition of his lips. God had to purge his lips from everything unclean. The moment the prophet Isaiah saw a glimpse of God's holiness, he was confronted with his weakness. With unclean, infected, vile lips, Isaiah feared destruction, and I imagine he was immediately drawn to his knees. He was gripped with anguish because entering the presence of a king and not following proper protocol could mean death. Isaiah immediately halted the process and said, *"Woe is me...I am a man of unclean lips"* (Isaiah 6:5).

Then the angel took a burning coal from the altar and purified the prophet's lips.

Regrettably, many times, we respond incorrectly when we see God; hiding rather than yielding (Genesis 3:9). Our God is a God of intention, and He came with the aim to purify. God's instruction is to lay yourself on the burning coals of the altar and allow Him to remove everything vile from your lips, your heart, your mind and your ministry.

HEALING THE WOUNDS

47

TESTED

The kidneys signified God's judgment and complete inspection of a person. In the King James Version of the Bible, the word "rein" is used instead of "kidney." In subsequent modern translations, the word kidney is eliminated and replaced with the words "heart, mind or emotions," which is not the accurate Greek or Hebrew meaning. Psalms 26:2 (KJV) says, *"Examine me, O Lord, and prove me; try my reins and my heart."* Psalms 7:9 (KJV) says, *"Oh let the wickedness of the wicked come to an end; but establish the just: for the righteous God trieth the hearts and reins."* The *International Standard Bible Encyclopedia* says, "Derived from Latin "renes" through Old French "reins," has given place in modern English to the word "kidneys." According to Hebrew psychology, the reins are the seat of the deepest emotions and affections of man, which God alone can fully know."[32]

Recognizing that God's sovereignty and immutability are not altered with time is essential. He will heal and process a prophet however He pleases, and He will never compromise on what He requires of you. Psalms 115:3 says, *"But our God is in heaven; He does whatever He pleases."*

My spiritual father taught me we are never without seed and that we are transporters of someone else's healing. In May of 2005, I was in an evening worship service, and as I was leaving, the Spirit of God gently arrested my mouth. As I was passing a woman in the congregation, I said, "I will give you one of my kidneys."

At times, the Spirit of God will speak things through you to which your flesh and emotions have not yet committed. I was a little rattled, but as the months passed, I thought nothing else about the encounter. In retrospect, I realized what was going to produce life in her was about to produce death in me. God was preparing me for the ministry that He had etched in my spirit while I was yet being formed in my mother's womb. He was about to release a healing anointing that would flow through my heart into the hearts, minds, and souls of His prophets.

HEALING THE WOUNDS

    A few months later, I received a call from the kidney donation program at UCLA and was asked to come in to give blood to determine if we were even compatible for surgery. When the results came back, the nurse said, "I have never seen such a violent reaction;" this meant the recipient, and I were not compatible for surgery. She continued, "There is another test that can be ran, but normally we don't offer it because it is very expensive." She still decided to run this test to determine if the recipient's immune system was attacking mine or mine was attacking hers. If her immune system was the culprit, she could be administered medication to suppress the reaction. The next test came back positive, so she became a potential recipient should her physician approve the medication, which was in short supply, five doses were needed, and each dosage cost $20,000. On February 16, 2006, she and I went into surgery, and the offering was complete. A prophet later came to me and said, "God said now He could trust you."

    Mine was an acceptable sacrifice. Eleven years later, the recipient of my kidney is alive, in ministry and flourishing. Since that time, I have seen God increase me with supernatural provision in every area of my life. The Lord made me four promises because of my obedience. First, He would heal ALL my wounds. Secondly, He would prosper me because He now knew that there is nothing I won't give Him. Thirdly, He would heal the wounds of the priest. Lastly, He said my anointing would stir the stagnate waters and end negative cycles in the life of His prophets. We cannot determine what sacrifice God will require of us; our only responsibility is to answer and obey when He calls.

    I have included a portion of my operation report to corroborate my story. It is one thing to hear a person's testimony, but it is another thing to see it.

HEALING THE WOUNDS

Documents for: STYLES, YVONNE

STYLES, YVONNE
Inpatient Operation Report
UROLOGY/General

Date of Operation: Thursday, February 16, 2006
Pre-Operative Diagnosis: Donor nephrectomy
Post-Operative Diagnosis: Donor nephrectomy
Operation Title(s): Left laparoscopic donor nephrectomy
Surgeon: Peter Schulam, M.D., Ph.D. (P18088)
Assistant Surgeon(s): Joseph Liao, M.D. (P16888)
Anesthesia: General

Patient Date Of Birth: 01/25/1964, a 42-year-old female.

Indications: A 42-year-old female evaluated by the transplant service and found to be a compatible match to a friend for living unrelated kidney donation. She was offered both a laparoscopic or open approach, she elected for laparoscopic. The risks and benefits were discussed with her including increased operative time, need for emergent open operation, bleeding requiring transfusion, infection, pain, damage to surrounding organs not limited to the spleen, pancreas, colon, or duodenum, damage to the diaphragm, necessitating a chest tube, stroke, death, neuropathies associated with the above, bleeding, infection, need for secondary operation. All questions were answered and she wished to proceed.

Technique: The patient was brought to the operating room and given one gram of Ancef following placement in supine position. General anesthesia was induced without complications. An oral gastric tube and Foley catheter were placed. The patient was then placed in the left flank position, being sure to pad well all pressure points. She was prepped and draped in the usual sterile fashion. A Veress needle was used to obtain pneumoperitoneum and a 5 mm visual obturator trocar was placed 3 fingerbreadths below the xiphoid and the left rectus edge of the abdomen was entered under direct vision four fingerbreadths below this. A 5 mm trocar was placed at the level of the umbilicus and an additional 5 mm trocar was placed. We began by incising the white line of Toldt from the level of vessels up to the kidney to the posterior peritoneum overlying the kidney The lateral spleen was incised to the crease of the diaphragm. We identified the psoas muscle caudally and incised Gerota's fascia lateral to the adrenal gland. A fourth trocar was placed off the tip of the twelfth rib, it was 5 mm in diameter, for lateral traction on the kidney. It was dissected in its entirety. We came down to the renal hilum and identified the vein, then the gonadal vein. We circumferentially dissected the gonadal vein, clipped it, and then transected it. We created a plane lateral to the gonadal, elevating the ureter down to the iliac vessels. We turned our attention back to the renal hilum to circumferentially dissect the artery and vein. There was a single artery and a single vein. These were circumferentially dissected. We lysed all lateral and posterior attachments. Up to this point the patient was well hydrated, she received 25 mg of Mannitol and had good urine output. A 6 cm horizontal midline incision was made at the pubic hairline and fascia was incised longitudinally. A 15 mm trocar was placed through this. Through this, an endo-GIA was passed. The ureter was taken, then the artery, then the vein. The specimen was placed in an endocatch bag, removed and prepared for kidney donation, immediately blanched with ice, treated with lactated Ringers. The midline incision was closed with #1 Maxon in a figure-of-eight fashion. The abdomen was reinsufflated, inspected for hemostasis, being sure to check the area of midline incision, the stump of the ureter, the stump of the gonadal, the bed of the kidney, and renal hilum, all

HEALING THE WOUNDS

48

THE STING OF BETRAYAL

Prophets will have to deal with betrayal more times than they care to. The last thing David expected from Saul was for his envy to open the door to betrayal. People love a prophet when they first come on the scene. However, as the prophet becomes privy to more information, gains the allegiance of people or begins to excel, his presence becomes uncomfortable.

On one of my ministry assignments, the pastor loved my presence, called on me frequently for counsel and made me an integral part of the leadership. But as he became entrenched in sin and the people began to lean on me for direction, what initially had been admiration and respect turned to disdain and disgust. He allowed the powers that be to remove me from my assignment, and I had to deal with betrayal as the entire scenario began to unravel. His final comment to me was, "I will never have another prophet in this house."

Many times, your assignments are not people who welcome your presence long-term. You will find that when you have been hurt and even after you have forgiven, you still cannot shake the anguish of what happened—constantly replaying the incident in your mind.

Perhaps, you are currently dealing with the pain of betrayal. Betrayal is defined as, "The violation of an expressed or perceived trust by a person or persons whom someone relies upon." I remember my first Sunday at home after my assignment ended. Once again, I was broken by the betrayal of a very close relationship.

As I matured, I learned that not effectively dealing with the pain of betrayal can potentially result in severe emotional trauma. Betrayal changes the way you react to your environment and the people in it, making it difficult for you to love, trust, and connect. Once you have been betrayed, you develop the "throw-the-baby-out-with-the-bathwater" syndrome. It is safer not to deal with people at all than to take the time to get to know someone and run the risk of being hurt all over again. Unresolved emotions in a prophet can saturate his ministry with hate and distrust. The very people you have been called to serve are the very people you resist.

The deeper side of betrayal is self-betrayal. Projecting and pushing our hurts outward and staying on the path of "what they did to me" is very easy to do. It is far more difficult to deal with "what I did to myself." If you cannot trust anyone else, you surely must be able to trust yourself. But what happens if you can't even trust yourself anymore?

I believe it is crucial after every assignment to evaluate how effective you were at doing your job. In that assignment, I felt myself savoring the position of being a part of such an influential crowd. As a result, I began to betray myself because I was not adhering to the code of ethics that is required for a prophet. I was not involved in egregious sin, but I was compromising my position by being too closely attached. A fellow prophet sent me an email which read, "God said do not get too close to those people because their God is their belly."

The remedy for betrayal is remembering why you were sent. Keeping this antidote in plain view will insulate you from betrayal without and within. Judas betrayed Jesus, but Jesus was so focused on His assignment that His response to Judas was *"What you do, do quickly"* (John 13:27).

49

PROPHETIC TRAINING 101

The road of rejection to the prophet is what I call "Prophetic Training 101." Rejection, which is the thoroughfare for the prophetic life, is a process that the prophet must get used to quickly or this abnegation can emotionally destroy him. The Bible says of Jesus in Matthew 13:57 (NIV) that *"A prophet is not without honor except in his own town."* Usually, the ones with whom a prophet serves at church or the ones closest to him will reject him as his gift matures.

If you do not become comfortable and familiar with this training methodology, life will become grueling. God showed me many years ago that if you are too familiar with people, you will change your message based on their opinions. You will prophesy what people want to hear rather than what you have been called to speak. Rejection is a necessary and crucial element in the training of a prophet because the result is he will not be afraid of the people's faces, and he will stand sure-footed as he declares, *"Thus says the LORD!"*

Abandonment is the root and rejection is the manifestation. Deeply rooted in rejection is your perception of who you are. Because prophets never fit in, they embrace a life of solitude. If a prophet does not understand that the call is lonely, he will begin to believe that something is wrong with him. If feelings of rejection can thrive and flourish, prophets will believe the lies of the enemy. A prophet's sense of self, love, approval, and affection come from God—not people.

If a prophet is not careful, he can very easily become bound by a people-pleasing spirit. The author, Bob Sorge, wrote, "Praise is food for God and poison for man." Because of the weight of the message, a prophet cannot be common or familiar. The closer a prophet's relationship with God, the more it can become distant with people. A prophet's message cannot contain any mixture. Scripture consistently demonstrates how lonely the prophetic call can be. Prophets had to be summoned, and they were often alone. 1 Kings 22 establishes that although the king had the services of 400 prophets, Micaiah stood alone.

HEALING THE WOUNDS

Unmanaged rejection can be the gateway for a myriad of spirits that can usher a prophet into a lifetime of bondage. Although rejection can be painful, it can also be a prophet's greatest ally. Rejection will keep him from being entangled in the wrong crowd—no matter how badly he wants to belong. Noah's rejection by his countrymen, potentially, saved his family and positioned them for God's promise. What if everyone had liked Noah, had agreed with his assignment and had come to help? This sociability would have probably thrown Noah off course, and his assignment could have suffered. It has been said, "Man's rejection is God's protection."

If people like you too much or you are hanging on the edge of your seat waiting for someone to agree with you, the time has come to re-evaluate the power of your ministry. If everyone loves you, beware. Charles Spurgeon said, "The church that the world loves is the church that God abhors." Luke 6:26 records, *"Woe to you when all men speak well of you, for so did their fathers to the false prophets."* If you are a prophet and everyone likes you, it is a sure sign that the enemy has entered your camp.

50

UNDERSTANDING REJECTION

As addressed in the previous chapter, rejection is important to the prophetic ministry. A prophet may be popular, but popularity does not translate into likeability. Rejection is not always bad and can be the very instrument God is using to protect the prophet.

Sabotagers

Often, God will remove someone from your life you refuse to relinquish. It doesn't mean the person is bad; it simply means that person is bad for you. God's view of our lives is aerial rather than linear. He knows where we are going and what we are supposed to do. Some people can do more harm where we are going than where we are right now.

Rejection Opens the Door

Rejection unmanaged can create deep-seated insecurities. A prophet's inability to cope with rejection early in life can create inordinate affections to ease the pain. I believe prophets, more than those with any other gifting, struggle with sexual immorality. You must accept that you will not fit in, and you cannot want to fit in so badly that you compromise your prophetic posture.

A Wandering Spirit

Prophets must resist the temptation to be nomadic. It is important that a prophet is anchored in a house. If feelings of rejection have not been healed or managed, you will resist God's pull to plant you in a house so that you can grow deep roots. You will uproot yourself prematurely. If you are healed, and you are experiencing rejection from the people around you, assess whether you are in the wrong place.

HEALING THE WOUNDS

Jesus gave gifts to men (Ephesians 4:8), so there is an element of New Testament prophetics, if the church is mature, that accepts you as an integral part of the ministry.

It's God's Message

When God asks you to deliver a word, there is always a backstory. By this time, God has set the stage and has already been dealing with that person. People can be very resistant because they don't want change; they want relief. It's essential to remember that they are not rejecting you; they are rejecting the message. Our responsibility is to plant the seed; God is the only One who can bring true change in a person's life.

Wounded Emotions

If you constantly feel rejected, then maybe you have not settled the issue of son-ship. God is your Father, and He loves you with an everlasting love. You are a son first and a prophet second. I use the term "son" because it is gender neutral, and it refers to inheritance and identity. When Jesus was discharging His duties to the Holy Spirit, He said, *"I will not leave you as orphans"* (John 14:18, NASB).

Adhere to Prophetic Training

You cannot let people's opinion drive you. Your message must not be influenced by whether the people will accept you. The core of your message is the people's obedience to God.

The Prophet of Prophets

Jesus said in Mark 6:4 (NIV), *"A prophet is not without honor except in his own town, among his relatives and in his own home."* If Jesus was rejected, likewise, you will be rejected too.

HEALING THE WOUNDS

Prophetic Validation

Persistent unmanaged rejection will cause you to question the validity of your call. As a prophet, you must be sure you are called and by whom. You must settle the fact that God called you—not man. Jeremiah 1:5 says, *"Before I formed you in the womb I knew you; before you were born I sanctified you; I ordained you a prophet to the nations."*

Prophetic Timing

Occasionally, God will cause people to reject you because He is not yet finished with you. Many times, I thought I was ready until God revealed another area I needed to address. He will leave no stone unturned and desires your complete healing and wholeness. An unchecked spiritual limp can become a permanent disability. Infection always spreads faster than healthy tissue.

Spiritual DNA

A common theme about DNA is frequently heard in the church. As prophets, we must make sure our DNA is untainted and void of defects. Just like gene editing can be performed in the natural, it can be done in the spiritual. If we continue to release infected DNA and interbreed, we are committing spiritual incest and producing spiritual birth defects and anomalies.

51

CHARACTER OVER POWER

You can be a functional prophet with poor character and zero authenticity. We have been called, not only as prophets but as believers to be conformed to the image of Christ, which is the predestination of every saint (Romans 8:29). This verse suggests to me that character is greater than power. Power without character is an accident waiting to happen. I have seen powerful men and women of God destroy the very core of some of God's people simply because they lacked character. Who you are in the pulpit should be congruous with who you are out of the pulpit. Author Les Brown once shared with me that one of the best motivational speakers he had ever seen, destroyed her career by who she was when she left the podium.

Exemplary character is a prophet's greatest weapon and defining asset. The most important part of a prophet's message is what is left behind when he exits the pulpit. When the prophet leaves the people, it is imperative he makes sure they are left with God's presence—not his personality.

The law of fluid dynamics determines that the wake of a boat is the region of disturbed flow downstream from a solid body moving through fluid or the condition left behind when something passes it. The wake of a boat changes as the boat gains momentum. Prophet, at what speed are you destroying or building lives?

Additionally, a prophet must recognize that spiritual and emotional maturity are both crucial and important. Immature prophets tend to over-spiritualize matters, which can complicate a gospel that is very simple. They struggle with studying the written Bible because they live and breathe the *Rhema* word and can grow very bored by simply reading. As addressed in a previous chapter, the Word of God is the final authority on everything the believer says and does. A prophet cannot prophesy apart from the word.

Prophets have a propensity to be very critical, and because critiquing is one of a prophet's weaknesses, he must be rooted and grounded in love. The fruit of the Spirit should operate in a prophet's life more than anything else. Based on the damage that can be done in the realm of the spirit through prophetic ministry, the prophet, more than anyone, needs to have excellent character and walk in love.

Morality, mental qualities, disposition, temperament, nature, and attitude encompasses character. Character is not what you do but who you are. Walking out the standards you say you uphold is vitally important. A prophet's priority is to be a son first and a prophet second.

The Holy Spirit spoke to me years ago and said, "You are not your gift." His instruction drew a very definitive line between who I am as a person and what I do for the kingdom. When a prophet starts thinking that what he does is who he is, he is headed for trouble. When he starts thinking that people are coming to hear him and not God, he is treading on dangerous ground. Ministry is rewarding but sacrificial. Prophecy is not about your touching the people but more about them having an encounter with the Holy Spirit.

Your gift is a mechanism and vehicle you use to advance the kingdom of God in the earth. You, on the other hand, are a son or daughter of God who is continuously being transformed into the image of Christ as you walk in obedience to the Word. I have seen many young prophets make the mistake of thinking that their spiritual gifting defines them, and sadly, they spend more time developing their spiritual attributes than developing character. As a Christian, you will spend a lifetime working out your salvation and crucifying your flesh so that you can be useful to the kingdom of God. When you misconstrue the fact that your gift and you are the same, pride can set in very easily and cause tremendous harm to you and the body of Christ.

52

RECOVERING FROM GRIEF

Grieving is a natural part of life and everyone will experience the effects of it. So, what is grief? Grief is a person's response to loss. Because I have spent the last thirty years working in the healthcare industry, I have seen the devastating effects of perpetual grief, depression, and sadness on a person's health.

Although grieving is important, there must be a limit on how long a person grieves. When the prophet Moses died, the people grieved his death for thirty days. Deuteronomy 34:8 says, "*Until the time of weeping had ended.*" The Word also reminds us that weeping may endure for a night, but joy comes in the morning (Psalm 30:5). Genesis 50:3 records that the people mourned the death of Jacob (Israel) for seventy days.

God does not want grief to turn into a lifetime event. Everything that dies must be grieved. Perhaps, no specific timeframe is allotted for mourning, but by biblical accounts, the time is not protracted and has an ending. Times of grief are necessary, but feelings of grief are temporary. Grief has its purpose, but it also has its limits.

Processing it is not specific to a prophet, but it is an important weapon for them to have in their armory since the prophetic life can be characterized by severe warfare, loneliness, and loss. These assaults can make healthy grieving virtually impossible. I experienced grief in some very real ways. I mourned the loss of my mother, grandparents, marriage, and child.

While serving, a ministry I had poured my soul, sweat, and resources into rejected me as I began to walk in my calling. I realized at that time, people's love is conditional, and their feelings can shift very quickly when you move into prophetic responsibility. Grieving the loss of that ministry was far more painful than losing my mother or child because the hurt penetrated my spirit. I needed several years to heal and come to terms with the devastation. My grief eventually turned into bitterness and resentment. I believe one of the reasons it took me so long to go through the stages was because I did not realize

HEALING THE WOUNDS

I was grieving. Ministry was a new frontier for me, and I had always believed, up until that point, that if you were doing the work of the Lord, people would love and appreciate your efforts since we are all working on the same team.

David and Job are the poster children for overcoming grief. 1 Samuel 30 records David's response to the attack on Ziklag. The city had been burned down, and all the women and children captured and transported to another land. David sorely grieved the loss of his loved ones. The Bible says, *"Then David and the people who were with him lifted up their voices and wept, until they had no more power to weep" (1 Samuel 30:4).* Verse 6 records that the people were so grieved that they wanted to stone David to death.

What was David's response? He *"Encouraged himself in the LORD his God"* (1 Samuel 30:6). Therefore, one of the biblical responses to grief is encouragement. The prefix *en* means "from within." David built up his courage on the inside. He did not wait for someone to make him feel better. He made himself feel better. The life of Job is also a biblical example that a person can come back from loss and still flourish.

You may never be able to replace a person, a job or an endeavor, but you can honor the memory by living a full life. In retrospect, I am grateful for the places that I had the opportunity to touch God's people. God is in the restoration business. I heard a prophet say, "When life does not give you everything you hoped, God will balance the books."

Another key component in overcoming grief is understanding the difference between a normal, balanced grieving process and a spirit of depression that will try to attach itself to the hurting person. One helps the grieving person recuperate from the loss with the passing of time; the other causes him to decline and sink deeper and deeper into a pit of despair.

Bitterness and loneliness are often associated with the feelings of grief. Excessive grieving also prohibits our moving forward, and the pain that was outward is now turned inward. It can manifest itself in some very destructive behavioral patterns as well as sicknesses and

HEALING THE WOUNDS

diseases. God's promise in times of loss and sorrow is His comfort (Isaiah 61:2, 3), and our grieving will end (Isaiah 60:20).

Without going through the appropriate phases, a person short-circuits the process. It's important to understand that this is just a model and it is completely normal that you can go in and out of these phases before you completely heal. In her book, *On Death and Dying*, Elisabeth Kübler-Ross defined the five stages of the grief cycle.[33] If a person does not grieve properly they will be stuck in the cycle. Most people, park at anger and may stay in this state for years. It is important that we complete the cycle and return to meaningful life. The cycles or stages of grief are, shock and denial, anger, depression and detachment, dialoguing and bargaining, and acceptance.

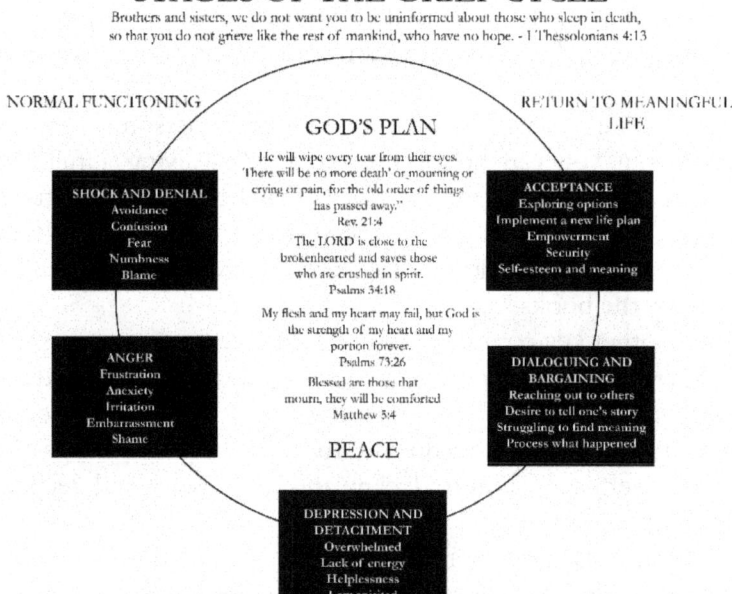

53

THE CLEANSING OF THE PRIESTS

The principle of the bronze laver is important for every prophet to understand. If a prophet is not clean, he will be self-seeking and self-absorbed. He will use the body of Christ to meet his spiritual, emotional, and financial needs. He will likely become intimate with a bride that does not belong to him. After all, the church is God's bride and does not belong to a prophet.

The prophet Joel urged the people of Israel to stop being religious and following rituals. Although God requires obedience, He wants a true inward conversion. He no longer wanted outward behavior from the children of Israel but desired and mandated an inward overhaul. Joel cried out in chapter 2, verses 12 and 13, *"Now, therefore,"* says the LORD, *"Turn to Me with all your heart, with fasting, with weeping, and with mourning." So, rend your heart, and not your garments."* God is more interested in a clean vessel than He is in an anointed vessel.

Many pastors today are teaching on grace, but grace does not make the wrong right. Grace is made available to us because of our human weakness, and God knew we would need it as we continuously work out our salvation.

The bronze laver was a wash basin filled with water in the Old Testament tabernacle, which had an inner court and an outer court. The bronze laver was positioned directly between the Holy of Holies and the brazen altar where all the sacrifices were offered to God. The brazen altar was a very busy place as thousands of sacrifices were offered to God annually. The priests washed after the sacrificial offerings in the laver, and before they entered the Holy of Holies, which represented God's presence. The bronze laver was a perpetual place of cleansing for Aaron, his sons, and their descendants.

> *Then the* LORD *spoke to Moses, saying: "You shall also make a laver of bronze, with its base also of bronze, for washing. You shall put it between the tabernacle of meeting and the altar. And you shall put water in it, for Aaron and his sons shall wash their hands and their feet in water from it. When they*

go into the tabernacle of meeting, or when they come near the altar to minister, to burn an offering made by fire to the LORD, *they shall wash with water, lest they die. So, they shall wash their hands and their feet, lest they die. And it shall be a statute forever to them—to him and his descendants throughout their generations.* (Exodus 30:17-21)

This principle is still applicable to us as New Testament priests. Our cleansing is now from within. As a prophet, you are still part of the royal priesthood and the holy nation that Peter addressed in 2 Peter 2:9, and as a priest, piety, holiness, and purity were not optional; the penalty for not meeting these requirements was death.

Every detail in the Bible was significant. An interesting fact regarding the bronze laver was the basin was made of mirrors that were donated to the craftsmen while the laver was being fabricated. Every time the priests approached the laver to cleanse their hands and their feet, they were faced with their own reflection; They *saw* themselves. Ministry requires that you look inward and then outward. Sanctification requires that we acknowledge our sins and frailties before we acknowledge those in others.

HEALING THE WOUNDS

54

THE LEPER CHRONICLES

And the LORD *said to Moses, "The following instructions are for those seeking ceremonial purification from a skin disease. Those who have been healed must be brought to the priest, who will examine them at a place outside the camp. If the priest finds that someone has been healed of a serious skin disease, he will perform a purification ceremony"* (Leviticus 14:1-4 NLT)).

Leprosy or Hansen's disease is one of the oldest ailments known to man. Originally, the term referred to any type of skin disease. It was highly communicable and was the AIDS of their day.

Dr. Paul Brand made the monumental discovery that leprosy, (also called Hansen's Disease), is really the loss of sensation to pain which makes sufferers susceptible to injury. Listen to what Dr. Brand has written, *"Hansen's disease is cruel, but not at all the way other diseases are. It primarily acts as an anesthetic, numbing the pain cells of hands, feet, nose, ears, and eyes. Not so bad, really, one might think. Most diseases are feared because of their pain – what makes a painless disease so horrible? Hansen's disease's numbing quality is precisely the reason such fabled destruction and decay of tissue occurs."*[34]

It is interesting that the inability to feel pain made the victim susceptible to injury. Spiritually, this gruesome disease can cause incredible spiritual damage because it hinders people from connecting to their emotional pain. If you are unable to do this, your emotions never heal because you keep repeating negative cycles causing more and more damage.

A leper is symbolic of spiritual pollution. The Old Testament contained strict biblical guidelines on dealing with an infected person to keep the population from becoming contaminated. As a result, those stricken with leprosy were banished to leper colonies. In the New Testament, the same principle applied. Historically, the wounded had to be taken out of the general population until they were restored, and their healing was confirmed by the chief priest (Leviticus 22:4). This principle must be applied to leprous leaders. Allowing them to continue in ministry is reckless. It is the same principle of sleeping with as many people as you can, knowing you have AIDS.

A primary focus of Jesus' ministry was curing leprosy, which in the eyes of the culture, was the deadliest disease. In Luke 5:12-14, Jesus reached out His hand and ordered the man to "Be clean!" Significant to today's culture is the permitting of infected prophets to lead. A leprous prophet must be sat down until his healing is confirmed. Since a prophet's call needs to be sanctioned and confirmed by a man, a better job must be done in confirming the true repentance or healing of the individual as evidenced by his lifestyle, eye witnesses and character.

HEALING THE WOUNDS

55

OFFENSES WILL COME

The word "offense" comes from the Greek word *skándalon*,[35] which means "the trigger of a trap (the mechanism closing a device on an unsuspecting victim, making escape impossible); (figuratively), putting a *negative cause-and-effect relationship* into motion."

In Luke 17:1 (KJV), Jesus said: *"offenses will come."* The word is plural, suggesting that it is a reoccurring event—not a one-time attack. You will be offended many times throughout your life and ministry. Learning how to handle these offenses is important. Prophets spend most of their ministry in the heat of battle, whether private or public. Because of that warfare, the enemy is always trying to discredit a prophet and render him ineffective.

If we are not careful, we can allow ourselves to be easily offended by the actions of others. Offenses create negative emotions that keep you attached to people who do not have the right to be in your life. God wants you to advance, but it is difficult to do so if you are offended. Be courageous enough not to simply ask God to search you, but to *let* Him search you!

Dealing with offenses was by far one of the hardest lessons I have ever had to learn. I had to discipline and train my emotions not to make people's issues my issues. If someone does not like me for no apparent reason that is not my issue; it speaks more to what is inside of that person. During the writing of this book, I had two sudden attacks that were unforeseen and unexpected. God gave me the opportunity to be victorious and thwart the enemy's attack through forgiveness.

The following is a prophetic word that the Lord gave me in the spring of 2012, but I believe it applies to the prophets and the body of Christ at large. He said, "The enemy is always working diligently to bring you to the place of offense, but we cannot handle this one like we did the last one. Deal with it and settle the score swiftly for too much is at stake in this dimension. The objective is not to internalize

HEALING THE WOUNDS

the matter because it is not personal! We do not want the enemy to sow roots of bitterness, rejection, doubt, and unforgiveness into our lives because we refuse to manage the attack expeditiously.

You've been through too much to be stagnant or lose ground. *"Great peace have them that love God's law, commandments, and statutes; absolutely nothing shall offend them or cause them to stumble"* (Psalm 119:165). The manifold purpose of an offense is to cause you to lose faith, tempt you to sin, knock you off course, cause you to take a route you wouldn't take under normal circumstances and make you lose sight of the goal.

Offenses almost always manifest themselves at the point of great transition; unfortunately, we have so many times in the past missed our opportunities because "we bit the bait." If you have been pressing into the kingdom and honoring your God, you are undeniably making progress, regardless of what it looks like. Paul said, *"For a great door and effectual is opened unto me, and there are many adversaries"* (1 Corinthians 16:9, KJV), and in Galatians 5:7 (NIV), he declared, *"You were running a good race. Who cut in on you."*

The counterattack is to PRESS! The word "press" means "to exert steady weight or force against; bear down, influence, as by insistent arguments; importune or entreat, lay stress on; emphasize, advance eagerly; push forward." Paul said, *"I press toward the goal for the prize of the upward call of God in Christ Jesus"* (Philippians 3:14). God has promised you hazard pay! You will receive "double for your trouble" (Isaiah 61:7)."

56

BLURRED LINES

The word "holy" is mentioned in the New King James Version of the Bible 576 times and the word "holiness" is mentioned 34 times. It is a theological thread that runs throughout the Bible and is one of God's immutable attributes. As a prophet of God, holiness is not an option but a command. The Hebrew word for holy is *qodosh* [36] which means "to be consecrated, set apart, distinct, different, undefiled, free from sin, pure, morally blameless and above reproach." The Greek word is *hagios*, [37] which irrevocably means "exclusively His." Can we honestly assert with no uncertainties that we are wholly His? Or are we like the children of Israel playing the harlot? Leviticus 20:26 expresses two immutable facts: 1) God is holy, and 2) He has separated His people for this very reason. Because God is holy, He needs nothing outside of Himself to validate His existence.

The bestselling and most controversial single of 2013 was *Blurred Lines* by Robin Thicke, which is the hedonistic philosophy of this present culture. This generation will not engage in any activity that will place boundaries on them or restrain their behavior. This post-modernist train of thought shuns the premise of absolute truth. To them, everything is acceptable. Only a fine line exists between the acceptable and the forbidden, even in the church and on the pulpit. The lines are blurred between our sexuality, marriage, the world and the church, religion, politics and every other defining principle.

The world no longer desires distinction but prefers *fluidity*, the "freedom to be who they are, what they do, where they go and how they live." The church no longer desires righteousness but religious activities that allow them to claim the name of Christ but live like the world. Our spiritual culture craves deep theological rhetoric and ignores the infallible, unchanging and irrefutable Word of God. God commanded us to be holy as He is holy in 1 Peter 1:15.

In 2 Corinthians 6:17, believers are admonished to, *"Come out from among them and be separate."* And to those who follow this directive, God adds, *"I will receive you."* The implication is that if you refuse to separate yourself from the world, then He will reject you and refuse to claim you as His own. Jeremiah 15:19 says, *"If you return, then I will bring you back; you shall stand before Me; if you take out the precious from the vile, you shall be as My mouth."*

Matthew Henry said, *"The way to preserve the face of the church is to preserve its holiness and purity."* The cry of the prophets has always been righteousness, holiness, sanctification, and consecration. Our messages neither change nor are they tempered by the post-modernistic culture in which we live.

Embedded in every prophetic function is the call to separate God's people to Himself, which is where Israel failed to hear the voices of the prophets. They carried on the external formalities of the temple, the daily services, the ritual and the liturgy. They adopted the forms and the vestments, but the inner life did not correspond to the outward. The constant cry of the prophets reminded them that the standard of God was still in effect. Continue to be the voice of one crying in the wilderness: *"Prepare ye the way of the Lord"* (Matthew 3:3).

HEALING THE WOUNDS

57

DIVINE CORRECTION

After serving fifteen years at a church, I was caught off guard when God told me it was time to move on. My next assignment was a start-up ministry, which was backed by one of the most influential couples in Hollywood. In about three years, the church grew from a handful of people to well over 3,000 in attendance. My family rolled up our spiritual sleeves once again and began to serve and connect with the people. Because the couple backing the church were notable Hollywood figures, the "who's who" of entertainment began to pour in.

I was appointed the director of the altar workers' ministry and had the opportunity to minister to, teach, lay hands on and lead to Christ some of Hollywood's elite. As I was entrenched in service, I received the following email from a fellow prophet whom I trust:

> A few weeks ago, you were in my dream. Then a few days after that dream, I had the same dream again, and the dream was to REMIND you of WHO you are! You are a PROPHET, a SEER, and God's instruction to you is NOT to become "common" with the "new" crowd you have been exposed to because it will compromise your position as a prophet. No matter what crowd or circle of friends you enter, you must not relinquish your position as a prophet. Do not be impressed by their status or by their names—because God is going to use you to "judge the people," and because of this, you cannot become "friends" with them.
>
> God gave you a "prophetic" break where the mantle was not heavy or a burden, but that time is over. A new yoke will be placed on you for the burden of the people you have encountered. If you try to become friends with them, fit in with them or become like them, your gift will be of no use for the kingdom. For though you are in the world, you are not of it. Also, be careful what you allow

your kids to be exposed to. Not everything that looks good is good. These people worship "other gods" (their career, money, and status), but God will not stand to be "another" god to them. He is the only living God, and that's THAT! 2 Timothy 3:5 (GW), *"They will appear to have a godly life, but they will not let its power change them. Stay away from such people."*

Sadly, the pastor eventually became involved in gross sin, and the church completely disbanded a couple of years or so later. I understood then that God was correcting me and bringing order to my skewed perception of where I was and the purpose of why I was serving. Proverbs 20:30 says, *"Blows that hurt cleanse away evil, as do stripes the inner depths of the heart."* (In this verse, *the inner depths of the heart* means "the rooms of the belly.") It is important to settle the fact that God will indeed correct His prophets. The correction of the Lord is an inevitability in the life of a prophet. Without it, He could not call us sons (Proverbs 3:11).

Learning to distinguish between condemnation and correction is important. So often we struggle with feelings of condemnation when God begins to correct. Additionally, many young prophets find it difficult to distinguish between God's correction and the accusations of the enemy. The apostle Paul wrote in Hebrews 12:6 (NIV), *"Because the LORD disciplines the one he loves, and he chastens everyone he accepts as his son."*

So, how do you distinguish between the two? Romans 8:1 (AMP) says, *"Therefore there is now no condemnation [no guilty verdict, no punishment] for those who are in Christ Jesus [who believe in Him as personal Lord and Savior]."* Correction uses the Word to chisel us into the image of God. Condemnation, on the other hand, mars God's image and produces guilt and shame. Correction is based on behavior that violates the Word of God. Condemnation is a false sense of guilt that is designed to criticize and punish its prey.

First, we must understand that God does not use His Word to condemn us but to correct us. Secondly, His Word assures us that the truth is designed to establish liberty. Lastly, the Word is used to free us

HEALING THE WOUNDS

from any indwelling sin (John 8:32). God desires that we flourish; Satan desires that we perish.

God will deal harshly with correcting His prophets because of the magnitude in which they impact the church. The enemy, on the other hand, will fervently agitate the prophets to silence the prophetic voice. A prophet will spend his life on the altar of the Lord under eagle-eyed scrutiny. Stay on course and spend time with the Holy Spirit so that you can distinguish between God's voice and the enemy's.

58

A SPIRIT OF ANGER

You cannot trust angry prophets. They are unstable and often allow their emotions to get the best of them. Interacting with these individuals is a constant discipline of walking on eggshells. They use anger to manipulate people and get their way. On the inside, they are shattered in a million pieces and anger is the only emotion they are comfortable expressing. Ecclesiastes 7:8-9 says, *"The end of a matter is better than its beginning; Patience of spirit is better than haughtiness of spirit (pride). Do not be eager in your heart to be angry, For anger dwells in the heart of fools."*

Prophets can have a proclivity to be very frustrated and easily angered. The prophetic mantle is a heavy one, and the prophet sees so much happening in the spirit realm that, quite possibly, it creates impatience in the natural. I also believe anger is an issue because the prophet's message does not always garner the human actions that are necessary to bring a person into the will of God. For example, if God prompts me to speak to a person concerning his drinking, and he refuses to take heed and dies from complications related to alcoholism, was the word wrong or did the person simply choose not to obey? A prophet must remember that results are up to God, and his only responsibility is to be obedient and deliver the message. A prophet cannot want more for people than they want for themselves.

Moses, the prophet, struggled with anger throughout his ministry because of the children of Israel's lack of spiritual fortitude. His anger cost him, and God did not let Moses off the hook (Numbers 20:11, 12). In the story, anger hurt Moses—not the people.

Anger is a serious problem, but the mark of a healthy prophet is emotional responsibility. Ephesians 4:26 (KJV) reminds every believer, *"Be ye angry, and sin not: let not the sun go down upon your wrath."* Anger in and of itself is not dangerous; it is the uncontrolled actions that are damaging. Scripture warns us not to even make friends with people who struggle with this unresolved emotion. Proverbs 22:24

(KJV), *"Make no friendship with an angry man; and with a furious man thou shalt not go."*

Psychologist say, "Anger can also be the offshoot of past hurts, injustice, and guilt. Unresolved issues cause pressure to build up in the soul of a person, which eventually explodes when a hurt similar to a past injury is triggered." If you struggle with this issue, may I recommend a book I wrote called *Get to the Root of It: A Guide to Emotional Healing*. This book addresses the fact that we assume the unresolved issues in our past will have no influence on our future relationships and how this thinking is faulty.

Other underlying reasons for anger is the pain of rejection and false accusations. As I have already mentioned, prophets deal with an abundance of rejection and are not the most liked people in ministry because they can expose people's wrong motives and ill intentions. This dynamic can create angst among the people with whom you are interacting, especially if they do not understand spiritual matters or are not willing to change. I have had several encounters in the marketplace where I knew a person did not like me merely because of my spiritual gifting. Many did not know what the issue was; they simply recognized that something about me agitated them.

Because I have conditioned myself to walk in love and represent God wherever I am, the injustice I felt produced anger, resentment, and bitterness in me. One company was so abusive that I could not wait to leave there. I was making well over six figures and had excellent benefits, but I could not endure the demeaning treatment any longer. After more than a decade of service, I knew the time had come for me to move on. I also knew I had to forgive those people before I left; God was not going to let me leave any sooner than that. I can say that the anger was still present, but the people were completely forgiven. I have had to constantly remind myself that justice is God's business—not mine. 1 Peter 3:9 (NIV) says, *"Do not repay evil with evil or insult with insult. On the contrary, repay evil with blessing, because to this you were called so that you may inherit a blessing."*

PART THREE

LESSONS LEARNED

Surely the Lord God does nothing, unless He reveals His secret to His servants the prophets (Amos 3:7)

59

THE PROPHET'S CREED

We are a new breed of prophets not bound or trapped by religion. By the infallible Word of God, we are breaking down every religious structure that is keeping God's people in bondage.

We worship the true and living God. As we worship, we are victorious over demonic influences, silence contrary winds and access the power of God (Psalm 8:2).

We believe that we are soldiers in God's army and no weapon in the enemy's arsenal can destroy our advancement (2 Timothy 2:3).

We believe in the power of prophetic connection and oversight. We understand that it is more important who we are under than who we are over (Acts 13:2, 3).

We believe that our words have power and every obstacle we face will crumble like the walls of Jericho (Joshua 6:20).

We believe nothing can compare to the efficacy of the blood of Jesus. It is a formidable fortress and an impenetrable shield that cleanses us from even the deepest of stains (Hebrews 10:22).

We believe a gift alone does not create a bastion for great leadership. Rather, great leadership is the by-product of a heart of integrity and righteous personal conviction (Psalm 78:72).

We believe the healing of body, soul, and spirit is our priority. We declare that we will lead a righteous and holy life with fortitude and dedication. We understand that Jesus bled *for* the people not *on* the people (3 John 1:2).

We believe God is moved only by the counsel of His Word. He is sovereign to the extent that He cannot be motivated to do good or evil (Psalm 103:19).

We believe the way into the kingdom is the threshing floor and the winnowing fan. Fleshly desires that hinder fluidity in the spirit must be cut off from their life source (Luke 3:9).

We believe God is a wellspring of life who enables us to live out our days with vigor and tenacity (John 4:14).

We believe our responsibility as ambassadors of Christ is to secure the presence of God for the people so that He can maximize the moment (Isaiah 61:1).

We believe the gifts of the Spirit were deposited in us for the sanctioning of ministry. We declare that the Holy Spirit will flow through us in power and authority (1 Corinthians 12:8-10).

We believe that God is strengthening us to live lives that are pleasing to Him. We declare we are committed to restraining from sinful behavior and understand sin causes us to be impotent (Ecclesiastes 10:1).

We declare that we will not offer up strange fire to God, and our worship is acceptable and a sweet aroma to His nostrils (Leviticus 9:22–10:2).

We believe the most effective church is one where people embrace the healing power of God and are fully engaged in the work of the kingdom (Matthew 11:12).

We declare we do not lust after the things of this world and that God's presence alone is satisfying and sufficient (1 John 2:16).

60

LESSONS LEARNED

History is the best teacher. The Biblical prophets were real people, although, at times, they can seem like fictional characters. The scriptures say, *"For everything that was written in the past was written to teach us so that through the endurance taught in the Scriptures and the encouragement they provide we might have hope"* (Romans 15:4, NIV). It would be foolish to ignore the lessons these men and women of God have taught. Their commitment and dedication to God's divine plan cannot be discounted. Indeed, the prophets lived in a world much different from the one in which we live today, but the ministry principles of God are eternally established, unaltered by trends or technological advancements.

So, what can be learned from the prophets of the Bible? Must we start from scratch or can we build on an already established platform? As a businesswoman, I know trying to reinvent the wheel is less than prudent. I would far rather operate a business on principles that have already been tested. In the remaining chapters, the lives of some of the prophets who walked before us will be explored. What was their assignment? What breadcrumbs did they leave for us to glean from and follow?

61

GOD'S NUMBER TWO MAN: AARON

The name, T. W. Wilson, is one that is virtually unknown. Mr. Wilson left a thriving ministry to serve as Billy Graham's executive assistant for decades. In his autobiographical book *Just As I Am*, Billy Graham reminds the reader several times that the ministry of the Billy Graham Evangelistic Association was and continues to be a team effort. Of those who worked with him, he wrote, "The dedicated men and women working with us have been willing to do anything and everything."

In his book *Leading with Billy Graham: The Leadership Principles and Life of T. W. Wilson*, Jay Dennis said of T. W. Wilson, "T. W. became the right-hand man whose wise counsel and dedicated service allowed Billy Graham's ministry to flourish. T. W. Wilson went on to greatly impact the world with his humble, purposeful servanthood."

Moses and Aaron were the first prophetic dynamic duo. God called Moses, and Moses refused because he did not feel his natural ability was enough to administrate the call. *"Then Moses said to the Lord, 'O my Lord, I am not eloquent, neither before nor since You have spoken to Your servant; but I am slow of speech and slow of tongue'"* (Exodus 4:10). God's response to Moses' resistance was for him to get his brother Aaron (Exodus 4:14, 15). Ministry is a team effort, and no one person can be successful in fulfilling God's call without a team of qualified individuals. I suppose that Aaron had his dreams that did not include following his little brother. His submission to God's plan is an invaluable lesson to every believer. Being the second man does not mean having the lesser anointing.

This social-media-driven world that pushes every person to be his own boss, to brand himself and to be the leader of the pack may well be creating crippled leaders. Therefore, you must resist the temptation to be the front man if you are called to be second.

62

COMMITTED TO THE CALL: AHIJAH

Jeroboam was one of the benefactors of Solomon's unfaithfulness to God. The prophet Ahijah declared to Jeroboam that God was going to rip the kingdom out of Solomon's hands and give ten tribes to him—if he walked in the ways of Yahweh (1 Kings 11:31). Jeroboam ignored the prophecy of Ahijah and led the people into idolatry.

Much like today's political system, the people who help get a person elected to office enjoy the fruits of their labor. In the natural, Ahijah was the catalyst for Jeroboam's promotion, which could have given him a special place in Jeroboam's heart and kingdom. But Ahijah was committed to the call. Regardless of the perks, he could have received; his first commitment was to God's original instruction.

The Bible contains many instances of men not wanting to hear the truth from God's prophet. Instead, they chose prophets who would tell them exactly what they wanted to hear.

As life progressed, Jeroboam's son became ill. Desperate, Jeroboam sent his wife, in disguise, with a gift of honey and bread to inquire of the prophet (1 Kings 14:1, 2). By this time, Ahijah was blind (1 Kings 14:4), but the Lord informed His prophet of her coming. Ahijah's message was a hard one for the queen to hear: *"When your feet enter the city, the child shall die"* (1 Kings 14:12).

Two lessons can be learned from the life of the prophet Ahijah. Sometimes, it is very easy for a prophet to become emotionally attached to the people to whom he ministers and for them to become attached to the prophet. When a person's life is drastically altered by the prophetic word, he develops a natural affinity. Ahijah's final message was not contingent on what he felt about Jeroboam; rather, he had to relay the message that God had commanded. A prophet cannot afford to allow his emotions to hinder his assignment.

Secondly, in his older years, the prophet Ahijah was unable to see and did not have the luxury of relying on his natural surroundings. Allowing yourself to be influenced by the expressions on people's faces or natural distractions can be easy.

63

FULLY LOADED: ABRAHAM

"Now the LORD *had said to Abram: "Get out of your country, from your family and from your father's house, to a land that I will show you"* (Genesis 12:1). Not only did God ask Abraham to move, but he also changed his name. In that day, changing your name could have been equivalent to changing your cell phone number today. Some people are going to get lost in transition.

From biblical accounts, Abraham did not look back as he obeyed God's voice. The Bible never mentions if he ever saw his family again. Prophetic ministry is not secure, and many times, you will be in environments that will pull you out of your comfort zone.

A study of the story of Abraham leaves the impression that Abraham and Lot were wandering through the wilderness alone. In fact, I have had that thought many times. But God made provision for Abraham's departure; he did not leave Haran empty-handed or alone. Genesis 12:5 says, *"They departed."* He left with his wife, his nephew, all their possessions and the people whom they had acquired. A woman told me something that I have never forgotten: "God's will, God's bill."

64

THE POWER OF PROPHETIC OVERSIGHT: AGABUS

Revival was breaking out in Antioch! Cyprus and Cyrene were declaring the good news of the gospel to the Hellenists. Acts 11:21 says, *"The hand of the Lord was with them, and a great number believed and turned to the Lord."* Saul's presence was requested to steward the work, and he taught the believers for an entire year. As the church in Antioch was growing, God assigned prophetic oversight.

Acts 11:27 and 12:10 mentions the prophet Agabus' frequent visits to Antioch. On one of the prophet's visits to the church in Antioch, he declared by the Spirit that a famine was coming over the entire inhabited earth. At his declaration, the saints in Antioch were moved to provide for their brothers and sisters in Judea. Acts 11:29 records, *"Then the disciples, each according to his ability, determined to send relief to the brethren dwelling in Judea."* Prophetic oversight is not only important to govern the body of Christ but also to unleash supernatural provision in times of famine (2 Chronicles 20:20).

65

READY TO MOVE: AMOS

God cares about what happens in a nation. He cares about the exploitation of the poor and political corruption. During the reign of King Jeroboam, the people were experiencing great wealth, which they attributed to the blessings of God, albeit this kind of wealth was the product of social injustice.

Most historians agree that prophets ministered in their own countries, but God sent Amos, a citizen of Jerusalem, across the border to address the debauchery of the northern kingdom. Amos came out of the cage swinging, and he turned that country upside down. Amaziah, the priest, told King Jeroboam, *"The land is not able to bear all his words"* (Amos 7:10).

Amos was minding his own business in his own country. He was breeding sheep and taking care of sycamore trees in Tekoa when God seemingly arrested him. *"Then the LORD took me as I followed the flock, And the LORD said to me, "Go, prophesy to My people Israel"* (Amos 7:15). Amos was not a professional prophet nor was he part of a prophetic company (Amos 7:14). He was a marketplace prophet who was earning a living. Something intangible about Amos captured God's attention and made him overlook the prophets of the day. Because of his character, God knew He could trust Amos to deliver the message without compromise.

I find it hard to believe, though, that Amos had not already been talking to God about this problem. He was already an advocate for social justice because his name meant "burden-bearer." I believe Amos was preparing for this very day.

Amos' story reminds me of an account I read about a shoemaker who had a burden for the nation of India. Every morning before starting work, he would lie across the map of India and pray for the nation. One day he was going to work as he normally did, and God said to him, "Today is the day." He closed his shop, headed to India and spent years declaring the good news of the gospel and winning many converts.

Toward the end of my corporate career, I struggled every day because my heart was somewhere else, but I knew I had to be faithful to the task at hand. God understands your burden because He gave it to you. Waiting on His timing is just as important. Pack your bags and be ready when He calls.

66

BRUISED BUT NOT BROKEN: ANNA

Anna was an aged prophetess who served God day and night with fastings and with prayer (Luke 2:36). The scriptures say she never left the temple. Anna was a woman on a mission, but she was no ordinary woman. She was the daughter of Phanuel from the tribe of Asher. The tribe of Asher was known to be extremely wealthy. Moses said, *"Asher is most blessed of sons; Let him be favored by his brothers, and let him dip his foot in oil. Your sandals shall be iron and bronze; As your days, so shall your strength"* (Deuteronomy 33:24, 25). In addition to their wealth, the women of the tribe of Asher were known to be beautiful and in demand for marriage.

Although Anna was a beautiful woman of means with a stellar pedigree, she was widowed and alone. A Jewish wedding, which was initiated by a twelve-month contractual agreement between both families, was a significant undertaking and a glorious occasion. The wedding feast alone lasted seven days. Imagine how excited Anna was and how she had planned a long, fruitful union only to be widowed after seven years of marriage.

Anna's early life was characterized by war and national oppression as was the life of another devout and just man from Jerusalem named Simeon. The Jews, at that time, were anticipating the consolation of Israel or the coming of the Messiah. The Holy Spirit had revealed to Simeon that he would not die until he had seen the Messiah.

> *So, he came by the Spirit into the temple. And when the parents brought in the Child Jesus, to do for Him according to the custom of the law, he took Him up in his arms and blessed God and said: "Lord, now You are letting Your servant depart in peace, According to Your word; For my eyes have seen Your Salvation Which You have prepared before the face of all peoples, A light to bring revelation to the Gentiles, And the glory of Your people Israel* (Luke 2:27-32).

Anna was in the women's court witnessing this glorious occasion. Seeing the Christ child was probably the second most momentous occasion in Anna's life; she could witness prophecy being fulfilled. I am sure Anna's plan was not to spend a great portion of her life alone in a temple, but she believed in the promises of God. She desired to see the Word fulfilled and to see the Messiah negate all the pain and anguish she had felt through the years. Anna was bruised but not broken.

67

GOD HONORS RIGHTEOUSNESS: DANIEL

God's righteousness is a recurrent thread throughout the Bible and one of His defining attributes. Psalm 7:11 says that He is the righteous judge. Also found in scripture is God rewarding the disposition of a man. 2 Samuel 22:21 says, *"The LORD rewarded me according to my righteousness; According to the cleanness of my hands He has recompensed me."* We have heard the word "righteous" many times, but what does it mean to be righteous? The word comes from the Greek word *dikaios*,[38] which means "observing divine laws or upright, faultless, innocent, and guiltless." Righteousness is seen in the person who observes God's divine laws. Daniel was such a man.

Many of the deeds of the prophet Daniel are very familiar. Most people know that he was condemned to a lion's den; he fasted and prayed for 21-days, and he was an interpreter of dreams. Yet, God saw something deeper in Daniel; He saw a righteous man who desired to be ten times better. Righteousness means "God's judicial approval." God honors those who walk upright before Him. God used Daniel as an example of righteousness to the prophet Ezekiel.

> *The word of the LORD came again to me, saying: "Son of man, when a land sins against Me by persistent unfaithfulness, I will stretch out My hand against it; I will cut off its supply of bread, send famine on it, and cut off man and beast from it. Even if these three men, Noah, Daniel, and Job, were in it, they would deliver only themselves by their righteousness," says the Lord GOD* (Ezekiel 14:12-15).

God appreciates our service and dedication to the work. People are thankful for a prophet's ministry, but righteousness is what sets a prophet apart from all the rest.

68

GOD'S LEADING LADY: DEBORAH

After the death of Joshua, the Israelites were still charged with defeating the Canaanites, thus honoring the covenant they had made with God. Following Joshua's leadership, the Lord appointed key military leaders called judges.

Deborah, the only woman appointed as a judge, was a wife, a judge and a prophetess. She was appointed by God to be a commander and a chief over the army of Israel. Deborah enters the picture after Israel once again did evil in the sight of God. The children of Israel were under the oppression of Jabin, the king of Canaan, and the commander of his army Sisera. Deborah established her office under a tree between Bethel and Ramah, where the Israelites inquired of her for guidance.

One day, probably following a vision from God, she summoned Barak from his home in Kedesh to assemble an army of ten thousand men to take to Mount Tabor (Judges 4:6). Barak agreed but was hesitant to go up without her. Judges 4:8 records, *"And Barak said to her, 'If you will go with me, then I will go; but if you will not go with me, I will not go!'"* Just as the people of Israel had relied on Deborah's leadership, so did Barak (Judges 4:5). As the army set out to defeat Sisera, Deborah informed him that he would not receive any recognition, but God would deliver Sisera into the hands of a woman (Joshua 4:9, 10). What an amazing scene Deborah, Barak, and ten thousand mighty men following them as they marched up to Mount Tabor!

Sisera's army was supernaturally defeated, and not one soldier of the enemy's army remained. Sisera fled and ended up in the tent of Jael, the wife of Heber. Jael gave him a place to sleep, a warm cup of milk, and once he fell asleep, she drove a stake through his temple. The event played out exactly as Deborah had prophesied. God started the battle with a woman and ended it with a woman.

The Bible first identified Deborah's function and then her marital status. This order is very important as it is difficult for a woman to lead without the support of her husband. Deborah was a prominent figure in her day, and the people relied on her leadership ability. In this patriarchal society, a woman was identified in relationship to her husband. This biblical scenario poses the question: how can a woman in ministry be successful in a male-dominated vocation?

Although Deborah had the authority from God to lead, she still had to win over the loyalty of the men. I believe the key to a woman remaining a relevant voice is understanding her position as a woman. We can lead successfully with grace and without discrediting the male authority. Jackie McCullough, a well-known pastor and spiritual leader, was asked the question: "Do men have a problem with your being in the ministry?" She answered, "No because I don't try to be a man." Femininity and submission is not a sign of weakness but a sign of power.

69

MENTAL EXHAUSTION: ELIJAH

One of the greatest confrontations in biblical history involves Elijah on Mount Carmel settling the score with the false prophets who ate at Jezebel's table. He issues them a formal indictment in 1 Kings 18:21: *"How long will you falter between two opinions? If the LORD is God, follow Him; but if Baal, follow him. But the people answered him not a word."* The God who answered by fire won and the 450 prophets of Baal were executed by the sword. Ahab told his wife Jezebel what Elijah had done. Her servant then delivered a message to Elijah. *"So, let the gods do to me, and more also, if I do not make your life as the life of one of them by tomorrow about this time"* (2 Kings 19:1). When Elijah saw Jezebel's message, he became fearful, emotionally crumbled and ran for his life (1 Kings 19:4). The operative word was *saw*. He envisioned his demise. God had defeated 450 prophets of Baal at Elijah's hand, but he could not handle one woman.

    This scenario teaches us about the power of psychological warfare. Elijah shrank under a threat. 1 Peter 1:13 admonishes the believer to *"Therefore gird up the loins of your mind, and be sober."* The word *"gird"* literally means "to prepare to move quickly." The prophet's garment did not allow him to participate in the battle. To facilitate movement, they would gather the fabric above their knees and tuck it into their girdle or belt. 1 Kings 18:46 is a depiction of Elijah's girding up his garment: *"Then the hand of the LORD came upon Elijah; and he girded up his loins and ran ahead of Ahab to the entrance of Jezreel."* Elijah was strong in his anointing but emotionally spent. Mental health and rest are imperative for a prophet because the battle after the battle is the one that can defeat him.

70

GOD'S SUCCESSION PLAN: ELISHA

The stage is constantly changing, and as the last battalion of generals leaves the stage, it is important to identify those who will pick up the mantle and run with it. Many of today's ministries neither understand the power of succession nor do they understand the responsibility of choosing a leader who is equipped for the call. Following Elijah's grand finale, God tells him to set the next ministry team in place. God's instructions were as follows:

> *Go, return on your way to the Wilderness of Damascus; and when you arrive, anoint Hazael as king over Syria. Also, you shall anoint Jehu the son of Nimshi as king over Israel. And Elisha the son of Shaphat of Abel Meholah you shall anoint as prophet in your place. It shall be that whoever escapes the sword of Hazael, Jehu will kill; and whoever escapes the sword of Jehu, Elisha will kill* (1 Kings 19:15-17).

Elijah obeyed the Lord and found Elisha who was plowing in a field and threw his cloak upon him (1 Kings 19:19). Throwing his cloak on the shoulders of another was symbolic of transferring the prophetic mantle. Elisha was positioned, capable and already managing his responsibilities. He could have thrown off the cloak and refused Elijah's invitation. Elisha's one request was to bid his parents goodbye for he knew it would be a long time before he would see them again. The Bible says then he followed Elijah and served him (1 Kings 19:21). He had no idea what his new responsibility entailed, but he was eager to learn. He also understood that Elijah's cloak was not his until the prophet died.

Prophetic ministry is important to the continued, progressive movement of the church. Choose capable people who are responsible, willing to serve and eager to learn to walk in your place.

71

DELIVERING A DIFFICULT MESSAGE: EZEKIEL

Some messages are more difficult to convey than others. Ezekiel was given the task of telling the children of Israel that they were going back into bondage, but that God would deliver them one day. Imagine telling your parents, siblings, children or closest friends, "You are going to spend your life in captivity." God's message to Israel is found in Ezekiel chapter six:

Indeed I, even I, will bring a sword against you, and I will destroy your high places. Then your altars shall be desolate, your incense altars shall be broken, and I will cast down your slain men before your idols. And I will lay the corpses of the children of Israel before their idols, and I will scatter your bones all around your altars. In all your dwelling places the cities shall be laid waste, and the high places shall be desolate, so that your altars may be laid waste and made desolate, your idols may be broken and made to cease, your incense altars may be cut down, and your works may be abolished. The slain shall fall in your midst, and you shall know that I am the LORD (Ezekiel 6:3-7).

Stephen N. Miller wrote, "Some scenes in Ezekiel are horrifying—with symbolic writing at times beyond comprehension. For these reasons, some rabbis banned the book for anyone under the age of 30."[39]

God is so serious about His message; He would not even allow the people to mourn. As a symbolic example of God's emphatic message, He strips away the love of Ezekiel's life and forbids him to shed a tear. God instructs Ezekiel: `

Also, the word of the LORD came to me, saying, "Son of man, behold, I take away from you the desire of your eyes with one stroke; yet you shall neither mourn nor weep, nor shall your tears run down. Sigh in silence, make no mourning for the dead; bind your turban on your head, and put your sandals on your feet; do not cover your lips, and do not eat man's bread of sorrow. So, I spoke to the people in the morning, and at evening my wife died; and the next morning I did as I was commanded (Ezekiel 24:15-18).

We can never shy away from the difficulties of prophetic ministry. God's message must take precedence over our fear or reputation. I was attending a church a few years ago, and I dreamed a horrific dream about the pastor being stabbed. I woke up emotionally rattled. At that moment, I knew the church was in trouble, and that message was one of the most difficult I have ever had to deliver. Because the pastor refused to repent, a church on the precipice of change and promise completely folded. God is not a liar and will stand by the word He delivers.

72

A KEY TO GREAT LEADERSHIP: GAD

David was ordered by God not to conduct a census of the people. God did not give His reasoning for forbidding this tally but required David's obedience to His instructions. 1 Chronicles 21:1 says, *"Now Satan stood up against Israel, and moved David to number Israel."* As a result, the Lord sent an angel who, with his outstretched hands, killed 70,000 men. Because of David's sin, the Lord sent a message to David's seer, Gad:

> *Now when David arose in the morning, the word of the* LORD *came to the prophet Gad, David's seer, saying, "Go and tell David, Thus says the* LORD: *'I offer you three things; choose one of them for yourself, that I may do it to you.'" So, Gad came to David and told him; and he said to him, "Shall seven years of famine come to you in your land? Or shall you flee three months before your enemies, while they pursue you? Or shall there be three days' plague in your land? Now consider and see what answer I should take back to Him who sent me* (2 Samuel 24:11-13).

David is a central figure in biblical history and even he understood the principle of accountability. When you have reached the pinnacle of your success, it is easy to think the only voice you need to hear from is God. Every great leader needs a prophetic voice, especially a voice that is not afraid to confront the leader and tell him the truth.

As David's assistant, I am sure that this pronouncement was difficult for Gad to deliver, but he was obligated to speak the word of the Lord to David. He was not intimidated by David's leadership or position because he understood that his responsibility was to God first.

73

IT'S NOT FAIR: HABAKKUK

The book of Habakkuk opens with the prophet interrogating God about what is happening in his nation.

> *O Lord, how long shall I cry, And You will not hear? Even cry out to You, "Violence!" And You will not save. Why do You show me iniquity, and cause me to see trouble? For plundering and violence are before me. There is strife, and contention arises* (Habakkuk 1:1-3).

Habakkuk is at his wit's end with God. He is completely frustrated by the injustice, violence, and destruction happening and cannot understand why God is doing nothing about the situation.

Many times, a prophet will have to watch innocent people, including himself, be mistreated. He did not understand why God was seemingly taking His time in addressing the matter. This apparent indifference on God's part is probably one of a prophet's greatest frustrations. Sin exasperates a prophet, and God's spokesperson wants immediate justice! Regardless of a prophet's frustration, it is vitally important to remember that God does not ignore sin, and He responds as follows:

> *Fret not thyself because of evildoers, neither be thou envious against the workers of iniquity. For they shall soon be cut down like the grass, and wither as the green herb. Trust in the* LORD, *and do good; so shalt thou dwell in the land, and verily thou shalt be fed. Delight thyself also in the* LORD: *and he shall give thee the desires of thine heart. Commit thy way unto the* LORD; *trust also in him; and he shall bring it to pass* (Psalm 37:1-5, KJV)

In Habakkuk 1:2, the prophet reminds God of His holiness to persuade Him to move expeditiously. "*You are of purer eyes than to behold evil, and cannot look on wickedness. Why do You look on those who deal treacherously, and hold Your tongue when the wicked devours a person more righteous than he?*" (Habakkuk 1:13).

Patience is a prophet's greatest asset because God will move in His own time and in His own way.

74

WORKING IN TANDEM: HAGGAI AND ZECHARIAH

God loves a good team! Although prophets tend to work alone, it is far more profitable to pool your resources and energy to get the job done.

After 50 years of being exiled, 50,000 Jews returned home only to find the temple in ruins. Upon their initial return, they rebuilt the foundation, but because of shifts in the political arena, the building was halted. The word of the Lord to Haggai reproved the children of Israel. *"Then the word of the LORD came by Haggai the prophet, saying, 'Is it time for you yourselves to live in your [expensive] paneled houses while this house [of the LORD] lies in ruins?'"* (Haggai 1:3, 4, AMP). Ezra 5:1 and 2 reveal that Haggai and Zechariah joined forces.

> *Then the prophet Haggai and Zechariah the son of Iddo, prophets, prophesied to the Jews who were in Judah and Jerusalem, in the name of the God of Israel, who was over them. So, Zerubbabel the son of Shealtiel and Jeshua the son of Jozadak rose up and began to build the house of God which is in Jerusalem; and the prophets of God were with them, helping them.*

In the natural, the prophetic ministry can fall prey to envy and jealousy. Humility must be interwoven into the fabric of a prophetic house to prevent competition.

75

A HOUSE IN ORDER: HEMAN AND SAMUEL

The Law required David to organize the priests into 24 divisions, so they could fulfill their duties (1 Chronicles 23:28-31), but no provisions in the Law regarding the temple musicians were specified. 1 Chronicles 23:4 and 5 record the following:

> *Of these, twenty-four thousand were to look after the work of the house of the* LORD, *six thousand were officers and judges, four thousand were gatekeepers, and four thousand praised the* LORD *with musical instruments, "which I made," said David, "for giving praise.*

David set apart the sons of Asaph, of Heman and of Jeduthun, who prophesied with stringed instruments, harps, and cymbals. Heman was the father of fourteen sons and three daughters, who were all under the direction of their father regarding the music of the house (1 Chronicles 25:5). Heman was the king's seer, which is equivalent to the title of a prophet. As the grandson of Samuel, Heman was a member of a prophetic aristocracy. As the father of such a large household, he was the leader of the ideal family. Nothing is more noble than a man who trains his children to serve the Lord.

Today's prophets must remember not to leave their children behind as their prophetic ministry expands. Samuel and his first-born son Joel are perfect examples of a father and a grandfather protecting the legacy of their family (1 Chronicles 6:33).

76

UNCOMMON OBEDIENCE: HOSEA

Once again, God had become incensed by Israel's harlotry—both spiritually and naturally. *"Hear the word of the LORD, You children of Israel, For the LORD brings a charge against the inhabitants of the land: "There is no truth or mercy or knowledge of God in the land"* (Hosea 4:1).

In Hosea 2:2, God not only reminded Israel about the present state of their relationships, He additionally brought charges against His people: *"Bring charges against your mother, bring charges; For she is not My wife, nor am I her Husband! Let her put away her harlotries from her sight, And her adulteries from between her breasts."*
Their list of offenses included intercourse with temple prostitutes, idolatry, murder, adultery, lying, and stealing. God's mercy never fails to amaze me. Even after everything the children of Israel have put Him through, He is always prepared to bring restoration.
When God spoke to a prophet, He commanded him to deliver a message with His lists of demands. When God spoke to *Hosea*, whose name meant "he has delivered," his first assignment was to marry a prostitute. Hosea was instructed not only to marry her but to have children with her. God said, *"Go, take yourself a wife of harlotry and children of harlotry, For the land has committed great harlotry by departing from the LORD"* (Hosea 1:2). Prophetic ministry is challenging but being commissioned and used by God is an honor. Can you imagine Hosea's heart sinking in his chest?
God spoke, and Hosea went. He chose Gomer who was known to be a prostitute in that region. They married and had two children whose names represented God's message to His people. At the word of the Lord, Hosea's entire family was about to become a public spectacle for God to prove a point.
Understandably, the business of prostitution flourishes based on the number of customers you entertain, so Gomer likely continued in her profession, making her an adulterer too. God once again lays a

charge on Hosea to reclaim Gomer from her former life to show the children of Israel what He was willing to do for them (Hosea 3:1-5).

Because Hosea's story is so extreme, historians find the account problematic and lacking literal veracity, instead believing it is a parable. It is difficult to imagine that God would demand such a tall order from an ordinary individual, but Hosea was certainly up for the task and should be applauded for his uncommon obedience.

77

A TRUSTED PROFESSIONAL: HULDAH

Jerusalem was divided into four quarters, and Huldah resided in the second quarter with her husband Shallum who was a keeper of the wardrobe. Nothing is known of Huldah's genealogy, but she operated during the reign of King Josiah, declaring God's judgment and His mercy (2 Kings 22:16-20). During that timeframe, prophets were frequently sought in times of distress, so the Nation's leaders could know what God's will was.

Huldah's name is derived from the Hebrew word *Chuldah* meaning mole.[40] The mole is a mammal that predominantly lives underground. Because Huldah is the only female prophet mentioned during this time and she had knowledge of classified information, she had to live a life of discretion. Some Biblicists believe Huldah possibly served as an official court prophet. Notably, Huldah's gate stone is the only remaining remnant of the original temple entrance.

The king sent Shaphan the scribe, Hilkiah the priest and others to Huldah to seek divine counsel concerning matters of the state (2 Kings 22:14 and 2 Chronicles 34:22). For the king to send his trusted leaders to her, she had to be a woman of character. She could bridle her tongue, and she was not a gossip.

The prophetic ministry requires a high level of integrity. Since a prophet will be privy to sensitive information, he must have control over his tongue. Proverbs 10:19 says, *"In the multitude of words sin is not lacking, but he who restrains his lips is wise."*

78

PROPHETIC SCRIBES: NATHAN, SHEMAIAH, AHIJAH, ABIJAH AND IDDO

One of the greatest archeological finds of the twentieth century was the discovery of the Dead Sea Scrolls at Wadi Qumran. The scribal anointing has been crucial in preserving the accuracy and historical relevance of the Bible. A document is not considered historically valid because a group of intelligent minds say it is; archeological evidence and manuscript authority must be verified. The number of manuscripts available makes it easier to recreate the original.

Homer's *the Iliad,* which is one of the earliest works in Western literature, depicts the bloody account of the Trojan War. Despite this book's historical value, only a few more than 1,800 manuscripts are available. At the time these numbers were documented there were 66,362 manuscripts available for authentication for both the Old and New Testament.[41]

A *scribe* was "an appointed official in the king's cabinet and responsible for keeping the royal records." An aspirant to being a scribe had to go through rigorous training. A&E's video and television book on the Dead Sea scrolls articulate the following:

> The ancient art of scriptural calligraphy is alive and well in the hands of *sofers*, the scribes that produce Hebrew Torah scrolls and other religious writings. Learning to become a scribe requires rigorous study and training. In addition, to mastering the craft of calligraphy and the scores of letters and symbols used in the Hebrew alphabet, the *sofer* must be knowledgeable about the hundreds of laws pertaining to composing and handling a Torah scroll and other religious texts. Because the Torah scroll contains the name of God and his words, the manuscript must be written with devotion and purity, and the *sofer* must be pious and of sound character.[42]

The scribal anointing is a key element of the prophetic ministry. The following scriptures demonstrate how these prophets recorded biblical history.

> *Now the rest of the acts of Solomon, first and last, are they not written in the book of Nathan the prophet, in the prophecy of Ahijah the Shilonite, and in the visions of Iddo the seer concerning Jeroboam the son of Nebat?* (2 Chronicles 9:29).

> *The acts of Rehoboam, first and last, are they not written in the book of Shemaiah the prophet, and of Iddo the seer concerning genealogies? And there were wars between Rehoboam and Jeroboam all their days* (2 Chronicles 12:15).

> *Now the rest of the acts of Abijah, his ways, and his sayings are written in the annals of the prophet Iddo* (2 Chronicles 13:22).

Accuracy and paying attention to detail was a must. If the scribe made an error, it made the entire document invalid until it was fixed. In addition to having such a heavy responsibility, the scribes also had to be holy. The apostle Paul wrote, *"No, I strike a blow to my body and make it my slave so that after I have preached to others, I myself will not be disqualified for the prize"* (1 Corinthians 9:27, NIV). A scribe could not even pick up a pen without possessing a holy character. The validity of their ministry went far beyond a gift. Gifting serves a nation, but holiness preserves it.

79

MINISTRY PREPARATION: ISAIAH

The book of Isaiah opens with him seeing a vision of Judah's impending judgment and future restoration. However, Isaiah's throne-room experience changes the course of his prophetic ministry. The prophet had a divine encounter with God's holiness and sovereignty. Isaiah's depiction of his vision reads as follows:

> *In the year that King Uzziah died, I saw the Master sitting on a throne—high, exalted! —and the train of his robes filled the Temple. Angel-seraphs hovered above him, each with six wings. With two wings, they covered their faces, with two their feet, and with two they flew. And they called back and forth one to the other, Holy, Holy, Holy is God-of-the-Angel-Armies. His bright glory fills the whole earth. The foundations trembled at the sound of the angel voices, and then the whole house filled with smoke* (Isaiah 6:1-5, MSG).

I have met many people who said they have seen angels. I will never discount a person's religious experience, but when I see how calm people are about the encounter, that demeanor does not always align with biblical accounts. As previously mentioned, my oldest son had an angelic visitation at five years of age and 25 years later he is still rattled by the incident. After Isaiah's experience, he was confounded by the angels' and in awe of his presence:

> *Oh, no [Woe to me]! I ·will be destroyed [am ruined/doomed]. I am ·not pure [a man with unclean lips; that is, spiritually unworthy], and I live among people who are not pure [with unclean lips], but I have seen the King, the* LORD *All-Powerful [Almighty; of Heaven's Armies; of hosts]* (Isaiah 6:5, EXB).

A prophet's first commissioning encounter with God shows how ill-prepared he is for ministry and how much he needs God's sanctification even to administrate the call. For that reason alone, I believe so many people run from ministry; they simply do not feel worthy.

The seraphim picked up a hot coal, purified Isaiah's mouth by fire and told him: *"Your iniquity is taken away, and your sin is purged"* (Isaiah 6:7). The life of Isaiah reveals that having a call is simply not enough. God called him, met with him, cleansed him and sent him. If a prophet goes without the cleansing, old sins and habits will creep back into his life, and his ministry in God will be short-lived. A prophet can still be operating a church or a para-church ministry but having that position does not mean that God is still with him.

80

YOU ARE NEVER TOO YOUNG: JEREMIAH

Jeremiah is only one of a string of prophets who must bring correction to Israel's constant rebellion. When God called Jeremiah, he tried to dissuade God from doing so: *"Hold it, Master GOD! Look at me. I don't know anything. I'm only a boy!"* (Jeremiah 1:6, MSG). Rather than responding in disdain, God sent him a message of comfort, letting Jeremiah know He understood. God's response to Jeremiah was as follows:

> *Don't say, 'I'm only a boy.' I'll tell you where to go and you'll go there. I'll tell you what to say and you'll say it. Don't be afraid of a soul. I'll be right there, looking after you* (Jeremiah 1:7, 8, MSG).

Then God touched Jeremiah's mouth and said:

> *Look! I've just put my words in your mouth—hand-delivered! See what I've done? I've given you a job to do among nations and governments—a red-letter day! Your job is to pull up and tear down, take apart and demolish, and then start over, building and planting* (Isaiah 6:7-10, MSG).

Notably, Jeremiah was one of the prophets who prophesied during King Josiah's reign. Josiah was the youngest king ever to rule Judah. After the murder of his father, he assumed the throne at the tender age of eight. Josiah was credited with reforming Judah's religious structure. He went through the cities and destroyed the altars that had been erected to idols (2 Kings 23:19, 20).

Young prophet do not allow your age to hinder you from being a vessel that God can use. The validity of your ministry is not age but God's hand on you. Paul told Timothy, *"Don't let anyone think less of you because you are young. Be an example to all believers in what you say, in the way you live, in your love, your faith, and your purity"* (1 Timothy 4:12, NLT).

81

A SEASON OF TESHUVA: JOEL

The land had been desecrated by four swarms of locust because of Israel's disobedience (Joel 1:4). Nothing was left; the land was bare. Some scientists believe the land could have needed up to ten years to be revitalized to grow plants after a locust attack. Israel was about to experience the greatest economic hardship in their history. In recent times, the country of Madagascar has experienced a similar attack. National Public Radio (npr.org) reported:

> A single swarm may be an estimated 460 square miles in size, and there can be some 80 million locusts packed into less than a half-mile square. They wipe out massive areas and affect entire economies. The FAO [Food and Agriculture Organization of the United Nations] estimates that in Madagascar, about two-thirds of the landscape could be invaded and 13 million people's livelihoods are at risk from the current swarms.[43]

Joel sounded the alarm and declared, "the day of the Lord," which no one would be able to endure. Even during all this destruction, God still offered them deliverance; He was ready to make amends.

> *Now, therefore," says the* LORD, *"Turn to Me with all your heart, With fasting, with weeping, and with mourning." So, rend your heart, and not your garments; Return to the* LORD *your God, For He is gracious and merciful, Slow to anger, and of great kindness; And He relents from doing harm. Who knows if He will turn and relent, and leave a blessing behind Him* (Joel 2:12-14).

God's response to sin is consistent throughout the scriptures, "return to Me." On the Jewish calendar, the forty days before Yom Kippur have been set aside for what the Jewish nation calls *Teshuva*, which means "to turn." God is holy, and He hates sin, but He always leaves the door open to those who truly want to repent. God rejects religious rituals as a penance for sin. He desires a heart that is wholly devoted to Him.

82

GOD IS SOVEREIGN: JOHN THE BAPTIST

John the Baptist's birth was a supernatural event heralded by an angelic visitation. He came from an affluent family. His father, Zacharias, was a priest; his mother was a daughter of the sons of Aaron; his cousin was Jesus. Concerning his parents, Luke states, *"And they were both righteous before God, walking in all the commandments and ordinances of the Lord blameless"* (Luke 1:6). He was destined for greatness from birth. The angel declared to his father:

> *For he will be great in the sight of the Lord, and shall drink neither wine nor strong drink. He will also be filled with the Holy Spirit, even from his mother's womb. And he will turn many of the children of Israel to the Lord their God. He will also go before Him in the spirit and power of Elijah, 'to turn the hearts of the fathers to the children,' and the disobedient to the wisdom of the just, to make ready a people prepared for the Lord* (Luke 1:15-17).

John the Baptist was a prominent figure in his day, and his ministry was revered. From his birth, he was known throughout Judea (Luke 1:66). He was not only a prophet but a priest and was given the responsibility of ushering in a new priestly order and heralding the kingdom of God. Zacharias prophesied over his son, *"And you, child, will be called the prophet of the Highest; For you will go before the face of the Lord to prepare His ways"* (Luke 1:76). Jesus and John met at the Jordan River when the time came for Jesus' public revealing.

> *When He had been baptized, Jesus came up immediately from the water; and behold, the heavens were opened to Him, and He saw the Spirit of God descending like a dove and alighting upon Him. And suddenly a voice came from heaven, saying, "This is My Beloved Son, in whom I am well pleased* (Matthew 3:16).

As Jesus continued in ministry, commissioned His disciples and fed the five thousand, John was imprisoned. He was angry, disillusioned, and offended. He even questioned the validity of Jesus' ministry although he knew exactly who Jesus was (Matthew 11:3). Sarcasm? Maybe.

This generation thinks ministry is a job more than it is a call. Many believe their excellent service should garner them some special privilege in heaven. Some believe they should live in luxury and be celebrated for what they do. After John's extraordinary life, his head ended up on a platter as a birthday gift—probably not how he thought his ministry would end. The believer can only be assured of heaven. *"We are confident, yes, well pleased rather to be absent from the body and to be present with the Lord"* (2 Corinthians 5:8).

ABOUT THE AUTHOR

Yvonne Camper's mandate is to help prophets excel in the marketplace, marriage, and ministry. Her expertise is in organizational development with an emphasis on the Prophetic. Engaged in ministry and business for the past thirty years, she has worked for some of the largest non-profit organizations in the country as well as being elected to serve on their boards. As a natural-born leader, she has spent countless hours training leaders and giving spiritual counsel in both the private and public sector. She is a change agent and a prayer strategist with a powerful gift of impartation and healing; her message is revelatory, transforming, and revolutionary.

Yvonne is not only a dynamic speaker but is also a prolific writer. In addition to writing books, she has also written for several online blogs, local newspapers and national magazines. Yvonne has a B.A. in Christian Studies from Vision International University with coursework in childhood grief, trauma, and loss. She is also a member of American Association for Christian Counselors. She is currently pursuing her master's degree in the same field of study. Her ministry affiliation and oversight is through the Harvest International Ministries (HIM). She is a wife, the mother of nine children, which consists of five natural children and four step-children. She is also the grandmother of five.

Yvonne is no stranger to pain and hardship, she is a survivor of domestic violence, divorce, she overcame the grief and loss of her mother and stillborn child. Through lives challenges, she has poised herself to overcome and win. Her peers know her as an individual who lives a sacrificial life of giving and service. She selflessly donates her time to community development and missionary work, both domestic and abroad. The culmination of Yvonne's benevolence happened on February 16, 2006, when she donated a kidney to her friend. As a result, Between the Porch and the Altar Ministries was divinely birthed.

Visit yvonne at www.yvonnecamper.org and follow her on Facebook and Instagram @ yvonne camper ministries. You can also subscribe to her Youtube channel.

OTHER BOOKS BY YVONNE CAMPER

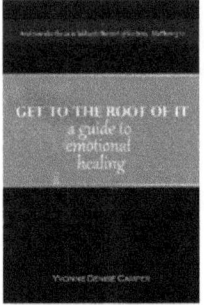

At Between the Porch and the Altar Ministries, we understand that your encounter with us is the beginning of the process. Healing is a consistent progressive effort on your part. We decided to develop this journal as a tool to aid you in continuing your journey to wholeness. Your deliverance solely depends on your belief that Jesus, by His blood, paid the full price for your redemption and conquered, on the cross, everything that can and will come against you. We think it is imperative that you chart your progress and the things that the Holy Spirit shares with you as you work through the issues that have plagued your soul.

There is an art to prayer and learning how to pray the way Jesus taught His disciples is the missing element to a power-packed prayer life. Our hardcover prayer journal is just what you need in your collection. You will learn the discipline and art of effectual fervent prayer. You will understand how angelic forces impact your prayer life and learn why so many people's prayers are ineffective. In addition to instructions on building an effective prayer, you will be able to document your journey effectively.

Geared for Greatness is a thought-provoking book about the things I taught my children; not only by words but by actions as well. Unfortunately, we teach our children more by what we "do" than what we "say." It has been quoted, "You never know what you taught your children until they grow up." I have made a concerted effort to teach my children everything I think they would need to know to make their lives successful emotionally, socially, and spiritually. It is not only a book but a workbook in which I have included daily affirmations to speak over your child as well as thought-provoking questions to aid you in gearing your child for greatness. We recently published our 3rd edition that includes a new chapter on Social Media and Your Child's 30-day Emotional Makeover.

WWW.QFPUBLISHING.COM

Are you interested in having us publish your book? Send us an email at
info@qfpublishing.com

NOTES

[1] Douglas Harper, "Holocaust," *Online Etymology Dictionary*, http://www.etymonline.com (accessed 25 August 2015).

[2] Warren W. Wiersbe, *Real Worship: Playground, Battleground, or Holy Ground?* (2nd Ed.: Grand Rapids: Baker Books, 2000), 16, 17.

[3] Bishop Clarence Mcclendon, *"Treading on New Territory,"* Sermon, Church of the Harvest, International, Los Angeles, CA, August 21, 1994.

[4] *NAS Exhaustive Concordance of the Bible* with Hebrew-Aramaic and Greek Dictionaries Copyright © 1981, 1998 by The Lockman Foundation

[5] James Strong, *Strong's Exhaustive Concordance of the Bible* (7th ed.: Nashville: Abingdon Press, 1890) Print.

[6] Strong's Anoint 5548," *Bible Hub, http*://biblehub.com /Anoint/5548.htm, 2011, Helps Ministries, Inc.

[7] Mrs. Charles E. Cowman, *Streams in the Desert* (Grand Rapids: Zondervan Corporation, 1996), 111.

[8] "Excerpts and Quotes From Dr. A. W. Tozer," *Sermon Index,* http://www.sermonindex.net/ (accessed April 15, 2017).

[9] "Strong's Greek 2137," *Bible Hub,* http://biblehub.com/ euodoo,/2137.htm, 2011, HELPS Word-studies (accessed April 15, 2017).

[10] "Strong's Greek 3126," *Bible Hub*, http://biblehub.com/ mammōnás,/3126.htm, 2011, HELPS Word-studies (accessed April 15, 2017).

[11] Douglas Harper, "Integrity," *Online Etymology Dictionary*, http://www.etymonline.com (accessed 25 August 2015).

[12] Strong's Greek 2139," *Bible Hub*, http://biblehub.com/euperistatos/2139.htm, 2011, HELPS Word-studies (accessed April 15, 2017).

[13] "Strong's Greek 5356," *Bible Hub,* http://biblehub.com/greek/5356.htm, 2011, HELPS Word-studies (accessed April 15, 2017).

[14] James Strong, *Strong's Exhaustive Concordance of the Bible* (7th ed.: Nashville: Abingdon Press, 1890) Print.

[15] "Undercurrent," *Merriam-Webster.com*, https://www.merriam-webster.com/dictionary/undercurrent, April 2015.

[16] "*NAS Exhaustive Concordance of the Bible* with Hebrew-Aramaic and Greek Dictionaries Copyright © 1981, 1998 by The Lockman Foundation

[17] "C. G. Jung's Theory," *The Myers & Briggs Foundation*, http://www.myersbriggs.org/my-mbti-personality-type/mbti-basics/c-g-jungs-theory.htm (accessed April 27, 2017).

[18] Ibid.

[19] Claudia Black, M.S.W., Ph.D., "*Understanding the Pain of Abandonment*," *Psychology Today*, June 4, 2010.

[20] Trauma, *2017 American Psychological Association* , May 5, 2017. http://www.apa.org/topics/trauma/

21 "Introject," *Merriam-Webster.com*, https://www.merriam-webster.com/dictionary/introject, April 2015.

22 "Introjection," *GoodTherapy.org*, http://www.goodtherapy.org/blog/psychpedia/introjection (accessed April 14, 2015).

23 "Codependency," *Merriam-Webster.com*, https://www.merriam-webster.com/dictionary/codependency (accessed April 14, 2017).

24 McLeod, S. A. (2016). *Maslow's Hierarchy of Needs*. Retrieved from www.simplypsychology.org/maslow.html. May 5, 2017

25 "James Strong, *Strong's Exhaustive Concordance of the Bible* 7 (7th ed.: Nashville: Abingdon Press, 1890) Print

26 "Wound," *Merriam-Webster.com*, https://www.merriam-Webster.com/dictionary/wound, August 2015.

27 From 'iy and kabowd; (there is) no glory, i.e. Inglorious. James Strong, *Strong's Exhaustive Concordance of the Bible* (7th ed.: Nashville: Abingdon Press, 1890) Print.

28 "root," *Merriam-Webster.com*, https://www.merriam-webster.com/dictionary/root, April 2015.

29 "root," *Merriam-Webster.com*, https://www.merriam-webster.com/dictionary/root, April 2015.

30 "Strong's Greek 2041," *Bible Hub*, http://biblehub.com/2041.htm, 2011, HELPS Word-studies (accessed April 15, 2017).

[31] John Watson, *"Sun Tzu's Art of War,"* https://suntzusaid.com/book/3 (accessed April 14, 2017).

[32] Bromiley, G W. *The International Standard Bible Encyclopedia.* Grand Rapids, Mich: W.B. Eerdmans, 1979. Print.

[33] Kübler-Ross, Elisabeth. *On Death and Dying.* New York: Collier Books, 1993. Print.

[34] Anderson, Brian. *"Cleansing for Spiritual Lepers."* http://www.thebridgeonline.net. N.p., 17 Mar. 2014. Web. 29 Apr. 2017.

[35] "Strong's Greek 4625," *Bible Hub,* http://biblehub.com/*skándalon*/4625.htm, 2011, HELPS Word-studies (accessed April 15, 2017).

[36] "Lexicon: Strong's H6944-*qodosh*," *Blue Letter Bible,* https://www.blueletterbible.org (accessed April 15, 2017).

[37] "Lexicon: Strong's G40-*hagios*," *Blue Letter Bible,* https://www.blueletterbible.org (accessed April 15, 2017).

[38] Strong's Greek 1342," *Bible Hub, ttp://biblehub.com/dikaios*/1342.htm, 2011, HELPS Word-studies (accessed April 15, 2017).

[39] Stephen N. Miller, *The Complete Guide to the Bible* (Uhrichsville, Oh: Barbour Books, 2007), 213.

[40] Robert L. Thomas, *NAS Exhaustive Concordance of the Bible with Hebrew-Aramaic and Greek Dictionaries* (LaHabra, Calif: The Lockman Foundation, 1998).

[41] Dr. Josh McDowell and Dr. Clay Jones, "The Bibliographical Test," adapt. from *The Bibliographical Test Updated,* Clay Jones, *Christian Research Journal,* Vol. 35, No. 3

(2012). http://www.equip.org/articles/the-bibliographical-test-updated (accessed April 17, 2017).

[42] "Enigma of the Dead Sea Scrolls: Extraordinary Revelations in the Discovery of the Dead Sea Scrolls," *A&E's Ancient Mysteries*, 1998, video.

[43] Jennifer S. Holland, "*Locusts Eat the Crops of Madagascar—and Each Other Too*," *National Public Radio,* http://www.npr.org/ (accessed April 17, 2017).

www.ingramcontent.com/pod-product-compliance
Lightning Source LLC
Chambersburg PA
CBHW071310110426
42743CB00042B/1244